Macroeconomics
for A2 Level

2nd Edition

Andrew Threadgould

Staff Tutor, Dulwich College

339

For S, J, P and C

ISBN 978-1-905504-71-8

Anforme Ltd, Stocksfield Hall, Stocksfield, Northumberland NE43 7TN.

Typeset by George Wishart & Associates, Whitley Bay.
Printed by Potts Print (UK) Ltd.

Contents

Chapter 1

The Economic Cycle

Fluctuations in economic growth

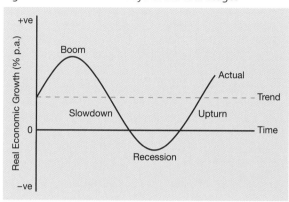

Figure 1.1: The economic cycle: the four stages

Economic growth is a key indicator of the state of the macroeconomy. The rate at which national income grows each year also affects other variables such as inflation, unemployment, the current account position on the balance of payments and the government's finances. The average, or trend, rate of economic growth is typically assumed to be 2.75% in the UK. Yet even in periods of stability, the actual rate of growth may fluctuate around this trend, and often dramatically so. This pattern is known as the economic cycle and is shown in Figure 1.1. It shows actual real growth in the UK since 1990.

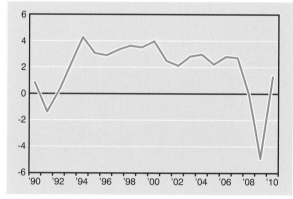

Figure 1.2: Real GDP growth in the UK (deflated using RPI)

Source: HM Treasury

The economic cycle is also sometimes referred to as the business cycle or trade cycle. During a boom the economy will typically suffer from increased inflationary pressure as increased output, incomes and expenditure feed into higher aggregate demand to drive prices upward. In slowdown and recession, unemployment increases as firms require fewer workers to meet lower demand for goods and services.

A key role for economic policy-makers (governments and central banks) is to slow aggregate demand down during a boom and speed it up in a slowdown. This is called stabilisation policy and helps the government and central bank to achieve the key macroeconomic policy objectives which can be listed as follows:

▶ Steady, sustainable economic growth

▶ A low inflation rate

▶ A low unemployment rate

▶ A satisfactory position on the current account of the balance of payments

▶ A satisfactory position with respect to the government finances/budget balance

Theories of economic growth

A fundamental issue in macroeconomics is what causes economic growth to fluctuate. Economists separate such theories into two groups: **endogenous** and **exogenous**. Endogenous theories aim to explain economic phenomena such as the economic cycle by internal events. Exogenous theories stress the importance of external shocks in influencing economic performance.

One economic cycle theory from the nineteenth century explained recessions and booms through the recurrence of sun spots. It was proposed that the natural pattern of different levels of sunshine dictated

the harvests of crops such as wheat. In a good year the output of agricultural goods would be high and food would therefore be cheap. Both the demand and supply sides of the economy would grow as households and producers both benefit. On the other hand, in years where harvests were weak there would be widespread poverty, even starvation. Economic growth would decline as both households and firms suffered from the shortage of food.

The sunspot theory may appear outdated now in an era where food availability (at least in developed economies) is rarely an issue due to capital-intensive production methods and where agricultural goods can be stored for long periods of time. Nonetheless it is a useful example of an exogenous theory: changes in levels of sunshine are very much an external factor to the macroeconomy!

We can identify four other explanations of changes in the level of economic activity. Firstly, changes in the levels of confidence; secondly, the multiplier-accelerator theory; thirdly, the stock cycle and finally the impact of shocks on the economy. We review each of these in turn.

Business and consumer confidence

Changes in the levels of **confidence** in the economy can have far-reaching implications. Both consumers and producers make spending decisions based on expectations of the future. If households expect their income to remain stable or even increase, and if firms believe that growth will be strong in the months ahead, consumption and investment will increase. The formula for aggregate demand is as follows:

$$AD = C + I + G + (X - M)$$

Where C = consumption
   I = investment
   G = government spending
   X = exports
   M = imports

For the UK, (C+I) accounts for well over half of GDP. This means that when both consumption and investment are increasing economic growth is almost certain to occur. Conversely, weaker confidence will lead to falling levels of consumption and investment as both households and firms reduce non-essential spending to adapt to more pessimistic expectations of the future.

The confidence theory of the economic cycle helps to explain how economies can move quickly from boom to slowdown. Data suggesting possible weakening of economic performance (e.g. rising unemployment or a decline in asset markets such as the stock exchange or the housing market) can be seen as evidence that a slowdown is likely. As these fears feed into lower consumer spending, firms cut investment. When combined with each other, these two effects reduce aggregate demand and the decline in confidence becomes a self-fulfilling prophecy. This theory helps to explain why politicians will invariably be as positive as possible about the economy – even in the face of clear evidence of slowdown or recession.

It can be argued that confidence can be both an endogenous or exogenous factor. In the case of the housing market, for example, prices are determined by a combination of market fundamentals (incomes, prices of related goods, levels of supply) and 'the animal spirits' of buyers and/or investors.

The multiplier-accelerator model

Two endogenous theories are the **multiplier-accelerator** theory and the inventory (or **stock cycle**) theory. These theories are very similar as they use the same mechanism for exploring the implications of changes in economic growth, but with different initial stimuli.

The multiplier-accelerator model combines the multiplier and accelerator effects to explain how aggregate demand can rise and fall dramatically. The theory hinges on the different ways in which consumption and investment change in response to national income. National income and consumption are positively related: as households experience higher incomes they increase spending on goods and services. The average level of consumption (C) to national income (Y) is calculated as C/Y and is called the average propensity to consume (APC). Of greater interest to economists is the marginal propensity to consume (MPC – not to be confused with the Monetary Policy Committee of the Bank of England) which is the ratio between change in consumption with respect to a change in income. The MPC determines the size of the multiplier effect: how an increase in national income (or GDP, or aggregate demand) causes higher consumption, which in turn increases aggregate demand, resulting in further increases in consumption. The multiplier is the ratio of the overall increase in GDP to the level of the initial stimulus; for example, if an increase in government spending of £10bn increases national income by £28bn, the value of the multiplier is 2.8 (£28bn/£10bn).

Table 1.1

Year	Index of real GDP (base year 2000)
2004	100
2005	105
2006	108
2007	108

Table 1.2

Year	Index of real GDP	Economic growth (% change on previous year)
2004	100	
2005	105	5.0%
2006	108	2.9%
2007	108	0.0%

The accelerator effect explains how investment changes in relation to GDP. Whereas consumption is determined mainly by national income, investment is determined by *changes in* national income. This difference is crucial, as changes in national income are far more volatile than national income itself. This can be seen in Table 1.1 where a hypothetical example is given (note this is not based on the data for an actual economy).

In the example shown above, economic growth slows over the four years shown. In percentage terms, growth is shown in Table 1.2.

Using this data we can show how consumption and investment may change. Table 1.3 shows possible responses by households and firms respectively.

Table 1.3

Year	Index of real GDP	Economic growth	Consumption £bn	Investment £bn
2004	100		500	300
2005	105	5.0%	525	330
2006	108	2.9%	540	340
2007	108	0.0%	540	310

Consumption changes in line with economic growth, and thus remains flat in 2007 as GDP fails to grow. Investment behaves very differently. Between 2004 and 2005 investment grows by 10%, double the rate of economic growth. As GDP rises well above trend, firms view the future with confidence and expand supply in preparation for higher consumer spending. Even in 2006, when growth slows to 2.9%, investment grows by more than this rate. In 2007, however, when GDP growth is flat, investment falls dramatically as firms choose to cease to expand and prepare for economic contraction.

Households have to maintain a basic consumption level (autonomous consumption) regardless of income: this is spending on necessities such as food, rent or mortgage and utility bills. Firms, on the other hand, can cut investment much more sharply. A retailer may freeze all store expansion plans or cut back heavily on staff training. This reduces revenue for other firms (the building contractor who would have built the new stores, for example, or the training consultants), which, when aggregated through the whole economy,

in turn leads to a slowdown in economic activity and thus economic growth and causes unemployment to rise. As the proportion of the workforce with a job declines, average household income falls and the multiplier effect will push consumption and national income downwards.

Thus the accelerator and multiplier effects combine to move the economy quickly into downturn. Table 1.4 shows the combined (C + I) value for the four years shown.

Table 1.4

Year	Index of GDP	Economic growth	Consumption + Investment
2004	100		800
2005	105	5.0%	855
2006	108	2.9%	880
2007	108	0.0%	850

With falling levels of (C + I) it is likely that, even with the possibility of growth in government spending or the current account, this economy could move into severe slowdown or recession in the near future.

Similarly, a jump in investment – as firms see greater business opportunities arise – will feed into higher consumer spending and an upwards multiplier effect. In both cases, the change in the rate of economic growth triggers a proportionately greater change in investment than consumption, but consumption quickly follows in the same direction as national income adjusts to changes in the size of its components.

Chapter 7 has data on consumption and investment in the UK which could be seen to support this theory.

The inventory cycle

The **inventory** or **stock cycle** (inventory is the US term for stocks) explains the economic cycle via changes in stock levels. Stocks in this context are raw materials, semi-finished goods or finished goods waiting to be sold (not *financial* stocks) and they perform an important function in the economy by acting as a buffer between production and consumption.

Very simply, an economy aims to produce the goods which are demanded by households, but the supply process is complex. Raw materials are extracted and processed into manufactured goods which are then distributed through wholesalers to retailers and sold to consumers. But as the exact demand for a particular good is unpredictable, at each stage of supply there are stocks. Retailers buy the supplies of, say, bottled mineral water that they think they will need to meet demand, but they will often overstock a good as demand may suddenly increase (e.g. due to a spell of hot weather) and they do not wish to lose customers to a rival firm if stocks run out. Similarly, wholesalers will hold stocks to cater for surges in demand from their customer: the retailer.

When economic growth is strong, i.e. during a boom, stocks will at first run down as consumers increase demand above usual levels and retailers see stocks fall. They increase their orders from their suppliers, who in turn will demand higher production from factories, who in turn buy more raw materials. The increase in demand feeds all the way back through the supply process until all agents adapt to the higher level of economic activity in their sector and stock levels return to their usual levels. However, if there is a downward change in consumer demand stocks will quickly accumulate throughout the supply chain. This may take time to clear even when demand rises again. This helps explain the persistence of recessions even when some economic indicators are signalling an upturn.

Exogenous demand and supply shocks

The models outlined above are good at showing how changes in confidence or household and business behaviour can quickly change the direction of economic growth. However, none gives a complete picture of how a recession (or boom) can result from first principles, i.e. *what causes* the initial shift in confidence or spending levels.

Exogenous demand shocks are external influences on the components of aggregate demand (consumption, investment, government spending, exports and imports) and they may result from a wide-ranging set of changes. They include, for example, a change in household taxation, shifting opportunities for expansion and profitability in the world economy and a change of government with new economic policies and attitudes to the optimal level of government intervention in the economy. Other possible sources of change relate to overseas demand (itself resulting from growth, employment and spending levels in other economies) or changes in the tastes for and relative prices of foreign-produced goods in the domestic economy.

Exogenous supply shocks are external influences on supply decisions, most typically those influencing the costs of extraction, production and distribution of raw materials, energy and goods and services.

Real world examples of exogenous shocks in recent years include (but are certainly not limited to) the 9/11 attacks on the World Trade Centre, the 7 July 2005 attacks in London and conflict in the Middle East. Other examples not associated with terrorism and wars are the growth of the internet and the rise and fall of the dot com industry in the late 1990s, the growth of cheap airlines, the expansion of the European Union and the fall of the Iron Curtain. Still more examples are various stock market and housing market bubbles and crashes, more open trade policy in China, the Credit Crunch and pro- and anti-globalisation policies by various governments. In each case, there are usually always both demand and supply-side effects and thus AD and/or SRAS and LRAS are likely to shift.

Demand-side shocks influence the actual level of (real) GDP in the economy and thus will determine the length and severity of upturn, boom, slowdown and recession. Supply-side shocks will affect both the actual and trend rate of growth and may therefore increase or reduce the productive potential of the economy. These factors will be discussed in greater detail in Chapter 3.

Stabilisation policy: managing the economic cycle

Demand management policy is used to control fluctuations in the macroeconomy over the course of the economic cycle. This is also called stabilisation policy and takes two main forms in the UK: fiscal policy and monetary policy.

Fiscal policy uses government spending and taxation to influence the level of spending in the economy, either directly (G is a component of aggregate demand) or indirectly (higher or lower levels of tax will reduce or increase consumption and possibly investment levels). The supply-side influence of fiscal policy is also increasingly being recognised as an important driver of long-run growth.

Monetary policy uses the price (the interest rate) and the quantity of money (money supply) to target aggregate demand. Interest rates, as influenced by the base rate of interest set by the Bank of England, affect consumption, investment and (see Chapter 5 for more detail) the current account of the balance of payments.

Figure 1.3: The economic cycle: stabilisation policy

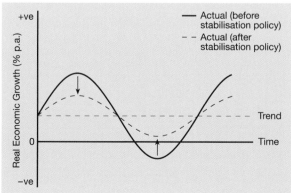

If used effectively, fiscal and monetary policy can even out the fluctuations of the economic cycle and move actual growth nearer to the trend rate of growth as shown in Figure 1.3.

Output gaps are the difference between actual output and potential output. A positive

output gap occurs when actual GDP is above the productive potential of the economy, and negative output gaps occur when actual GDP is below the productive potential. Output gaps (both positive and negative) are smaller in both boom and recession after successful intervention, but demand management policy is much more difficult in practice than theory.

Limitations on the effectiveness of demand management policy

There are several reasons why the use of stabilisation policies in practice encounter problems.

Government failure and time lags (fiscal and monetary policy)

Government failure arises when intervention fails to increase, or actually decreases, social welfare. This may arise if policies aimed at improving macroeconomic performance fail to do so. Imperfect information regarding the performance of the economy can result in inappropriate policy, and this can be exacerbated by sudden changes in the economy such as those resulting from exogenous shocks. If there is a belief that the economy is growing strongly then tighter demand management policy will be applied to slow down growth and dampen inflationary pressures. However, if growth slows of its own accord due to internal or external factors, the higher taxes and interest rates may bite just as the economy requires the opposite policy.

Both fiscal and monetary policies involve **time lags** between the identification of a problem, the implementation of an appropriate policy, and the full impact of that policy instrument on output, jobs and prices.

Financial disintermediation (monetary policy)

A problem specific to monetary policy in an increasingly globalised world is that of **disintermediation** in credit markets. Disintermediation occurs when middlemen in a supply chain are removed, increasing the transparency of a market. In credit markets the price of debt is the interest rate, and domestic monetary policy depends on the careful control of interest rates, via the base rate. Thus if inflation in the UK is increasing the Bank of England will raise the base rate. This increases the cost of borrowing for UK banks, who in turn can pass on this higher cost to households and firms in commercial rates of interest on loans.

However, UK banks can increasingly borrow money from foreign lenders where rates will be determined by foreign base rates. Thus greater competition in global credit markets reduces the power of domestic policy making.

The constraints of fiscal rules

In the UK the **golden rule** limited current government spending to tax receipts over the course of one economic cycle. The **sustainable investment rule** limited capital spending to a level which will not see national debt rise above 40% of GDP. In the Eurozone the **Stability and Growth Pact** limits a country's budget deficit to a maximum of 3% of GDP and national debt to a maximum of 60% of GDP. Experiences of both the UK (which suspended its own fiscal rules in light of the recent recession) and the Eurozone (which made the Stability and Growth Pact more flexible in 2005, but has been forced to accept breaches of its rules by even some of the stronger European economies) have brought into question the usefulness of such constraints. The key criticism is that authorities will adhere to rules until it is convenient for them to be broken!

The constraints of taxation principles

Fiscal policy may be constrained by its impact on society and perceptions of 'fairness' and 'value for money' from public services. Most people consider a progressive tax (where, as income rises, a higher proportion is paid in tax) as more desirable than a regressive tax (where, as income rises, the proportion paid in tax declines). We can refer to an effective tax as one which is fair (related to ability to pay) and economic to collect (administrative costs do not exceed the revenue generated). On a wider level, it might be useful to consider the 4R's of taxation: representation (accountability on the part of the Treasury to use

Governments often find it easier to justify tax increases on demerit goods such as alcohol, cigarettes and petrol.

funds fairly and effectively), repricing (correcting for externalities), redistribution (higher income households can afford to pay taxes more, and require the help of government less, than poorer households) and revenue (funding public expenditure). These facets of taxation hamper full freedom to deploy fiscal policy. Moreover changes in levels of spending and taxation will rarely affect all households and firms equally and thus the pattern of fiscal policy can affect certain groups as much as the overall fiscal position.

Governments often find it easier to justify tax increases if they are imposed on demerit goods such as alcohol, cigarettes and petrol. But relying on these goods to raise indirect taxation may distort patterns of expenditure and economic activity, and may even harm the macroeconomy if the good being taxed more heavily is exported, for example.

Direct taxation (income taxes) is the most important source of tax revenue in the UK. Changes in the level of income tax have influences on both a microeconomic and macroeconomic level. If the top rate of income tax was raised, for example, to increase funding to the NHS, this would help to redistribute income at the expense of slower economic growth. The microeconomic impact, however, could involve higher levels of employment in the NHS (more jobs for doctors, nurses and other staff) and job creation and higher profits for suppliers of drugs and medical equipment. In contrast, businesses depending on spending by the higher income households who are now paying more tax may suffer, for example swimming pool manufacturers or luxury car showrooms. This illustrates how a change in government spending or taxation may impact on the private sector such that the intended change in aggregate demand is not realised.

Crowding out

Crowding out is a controversial theory which examines the impact of looser fiscal control on the economy. It explores the impact of higher government spending on the economy, and in particular the effect on investment. With respect to the formula for aggregate demand earlier in the Chapter, the argument is that higher G may actually reduce I, thus negating the fiscal expansion. Crowding out provides a critique of 'bigger government': put simply, an increase in government activity in the economy reduces the opportunities for private investment.

Closely related to the concept of crowding out is *'crowding in'*. This is the theory that tighter fiscal discipline in the form of lower government spending can actually boost the economy through creating stronger incentives for private investment. Both of these concepts argue in favour of smaller government.

Summary questions

1. What problems are caused by fluctuations in the level of aggregate demand in the economy?

2. Explain the importance of confidence in the macroeconomy.

3. Distinguish between the multiplier effect and the accelerator effect and show how changes in the level of economic activity may have different impacts on consumption and investment.

4. What are exogenous shocks? Give an example of one demand-side and one supply-side shock from recent years.

5. Summarise the key limitations in using monetary and fiscal policy to control the macroeconomy.

Extension questions

A. What theory (or combination of theories) do you believe best explains the phenomenon of the economic cycle?

B. There is an argument that the 'economic cycle' is no more than a coincidence of periodic adjustments to external events – and thus not a regular cycle at all. To what extent do you agree with this point of view? What evidence may support this argument?

C. To what extent will the proposed cuts to government spending lead to stronger growth in the UK in the years ahead?

Chapter 2

Policy Conflict in the Macroeconomy

Macroeconomic management is constrained by policy conflict: changes in policy to influence one macroeconomic target can have knock-on effects on others. The main macroeconomic objectives of government were identified in the previous chapter.

Inflation and unemployment

One of the key policy conflicts in macroeconomics is that between inflation and unemployment. This relationship has for many years been the subject of much debate. Inflation tends to rise when there is strong growth in aggregate demand (demand-pull inflation) and firms face shortages of factors of production (resulting in higher factor prices and thus cost-push inflation) and some of these higher costs will be passed onto consumers. In addition, households demand higher incomes to maintain the real value of their earnings. In extreme cases the interplay of higher prices and higher costs gets out of hand and a wage-price spiral results.

Figure 2.1: The Phillips Curve

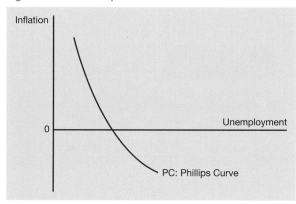

Unemployment increases when aggregate demand is growing below trend and thus demand-deficient or cyclical unemployment is closely linked to downturn or recession.

It appears that the relationship between inflation and unemployment is therefore negative: as the economy grows more quickly, we expect to see higher inflation and lower unemployment. Hence there is a trade-off between inflation and unemployment and this relationship was first formalised in the Phillips Curve as shown in Figure 2.1

Figure 2.2: The Long Run AS Curve

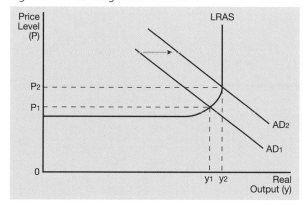

Throughout the 1950s and 1960s Keynesian economists believed that governments could choose between low inflation and low unemployment – or a compromise point in the middle. Fluctuations in the level of aggregate demand (the economic cycle) would cause movements along the curve, but these changes could be controlled with demand-side policies such as fiscal and monetary policy. Given the Keynesian Long Run Aggregate Supply curve, higher aggregate demand leads to higher real output

and falling unemployment is accompanied by rising inflationary pressure as shown in Figure 2.2. It was therefore the role of government to use demand management measures – fiscal and monetary policy – to move the economy to the desired point on the Phillips Curve.

However, the Phillips Curve trade-off appeared to break down in the 1970s in major economies such as the UK and USA. Whereas the post-war period had been a time where economies suffered from the threat of high inflation or high unemployment, a combination of factors created the simultaneous pressures of

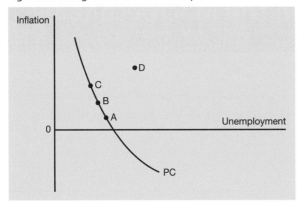

Figure 2.3: Stagflation and the Phillips Curve

Figure 2.4: The Monetarist view

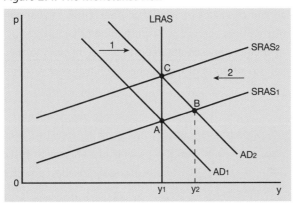

higher inflation and higher unemployment. Such a scenario is known as **stagflation** – a stagnant economy (low or negative growth, with high unemployment) combined with high inflation.

On Figure 2.3 points A, B and C represent combinations of inflation and unemployment which correspond to the trade-off position described above in the Phillips Curve. But when both variables increase there is a movement away from the curve – say to point D on the diagram. So the Phillips relationship would then no longer seem a robust one.

The post-war Keynesian consensus came under real scrutiny in the 1970s. The key figure in the anti-Keynesian school was Professor Milton Friedman at the University of Chicago who became synonymous with the Monetarist school. **Monetarists** (a term used loosely along with Supply-Siders and Neo-Classicists) argued that the 1950s and 1960s had been characterised by governments running budget deficits to fund public expenditure, and this had inevitably led to inflation. The Keynesian school had argued that higher aggregate demand resulting from loose fiscal and monetary policies may have allowed inflation to occur but this was offset by the benefits of lower unemployment. The Monetarist school, however, argued that in the long-run the only consequence of expansionary demand policies was high inflation.

Starting at point A in Figure 2.4, an increase in aggregate demand from AD1 to AD2 may be caused by either government policy (budget deficit or lower interest rates) or a boom in the economy. In the short-run this increases real output from y1 to y2, opening an output gap (the difference between actual GDP, y2, and potential GDP, y1). However, the Classical or Monetarist school would argue that this increase in real output pushes up prices as bottlenecks occur in the economy. There are shortages of factors of production, particularly labour, and this pushes up wages, rents, energy costs and raw material prices. This upward pressure on costs forces the short-run aggregate supply curve upwards from SRAS1 to SRAS2. Wages will rise until real output and unemployment return to their original levels at y1.

The movement from point A to B on Figure 2.4 represents an increase in inflation (an increase in the price level from p1 to p2) and a fall in unemployment. This appears to support the picture of the macroeconomy represented on the conventional Phillips Curve. However, the Monetarists would argue that point B is not sustainable in the short-run: in the long-run the economy moves back to point C. This combination of short-run and long-run positions is represented by the Short-Run Phillips Curve (SRPC) and Long-Run Phillips Curve (LRPC). Points A, B and C on Figure 2.5 are equivalent to the points on Figure 2.4, and LRPC – like LRAS – is vertical.

For the Monetarists, therefore, as with the Classical Model, the long-run real output level is determined entirely by supply-side factors: factor productivity and the incentives given to households and firms to supply labour and enterprise to the economy.

Demand management policy and the LRPC

Figure 2.5: The Long Run Phillips Curve

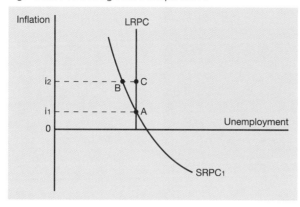

Stagflation in the 1970s seemed to be explained using the Monetarist view of the economy. If the government decides to reduce unemployment they can use expansionary fiscal policy (lower taxes and/or higher government spending) or expansionary monetary policy (lower interest rates and/or higher money supply), both of which will hopefully increase consumption and investment. But, building on Figure 2.5, this will increase inflation and reduce unemployment, but only in the short-run. Figure 2.6 shows how increasing AD will push SRPC1 out to SRPC2 in the long-run.

Figure 2.6: Short Run Phillips Curves

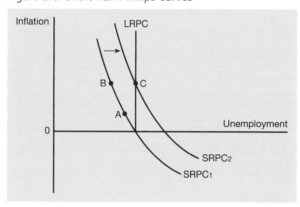

This view is linked to the Monetarist interpretation of the Fisher Equation, also known as the Quantity Theory of Money. It is given (regardless of economic philosophy) that the following identity is true:

$$MV = PT$$

M is the money supply (in simple terms, the total value of notes and coins in circulation), V is the velocity of circulation (the number of times a given note or coin changes hands in, say, one year), P is the price level (the average price goods and services are traded for) and T is the number of transactions (effectively, the real output of the economy, or y).

According to the Monetarists, V and T are constant. This means that any increase in money supply – such as printing money to fund higher government spending – will directly feed into higher prices. In the words of Milton Friedman, 'inflation is always and everywhere a monetary phenomenon'. Yet the assumption that V and T are constant is itself controversial. If even one of these variables is allowed to change – say, T – it can be shown that an increase in the level of money in the economy can have one of three impacts, rather than just one. These changes are shown below:

1. Constant P, higher T
2. Higher P and higher T
3. Higher P and constant T

Figure 2.7: The Keynesian Curve

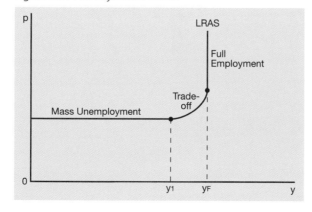

If the number of transactions is equivalent to real output (both measure the quantity of goods and services traded over a given period of time) these differing outcomes can be represented on the Keynesian view of the Long-Run Aggregate Supply Curve as shown in Figure 2.7

The flat section of the curve (mass unemployment) shows that real output can grow with no increase in prices. As the economy nears full employment there is an increasing

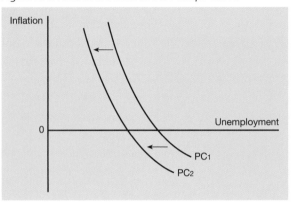

Figure 2.8: A leftward shift in the Phillips Curve

trade-off between higher real output and higher prices, until at full employment (yF) any attempt to increase real output will be unsuccessful, only resulting in higher prices.

The Keynesian riposte to the Monetarist critique of the Phillips curve is that stagflation results from supply-side rather than demand-related pressures. Thus when supply-side growth is low and costs are rising (for example, due to oil crises or high levels of trade union power) the Phillips Curve will shift outwards; similarly, supply-side growth (e.g. due to technological innovation or higher labour market participation) can move the Phillips Curve inwards – as shown in Figure 2.8.

A shift in the Short Run Phillips Curve

The early 1980s were a fascinating period for economists (if a very difficult time for many of the people living at the sharp end of the economy) as the competing ideologies of Keynesians and Monetarists competed to explain the difficulties experienced in Western Europe and the USA. On both sides of the Atlantic there were governments which adopted the views of Friedman and his followers; in the UK, this was known as **Thatcherism** and, in the USA, **Reaganomics**.

If inflation was seen as a monetary phenomenon, the cure for inflation was to reduce monetary expectations. In the UK, after years of strong trade union power which pushed up costs and reduced productivity, the Thatcher government systematically reduced trade union power at the same time as operating tight monetary and fiscal policies. As aggregate demand slowed, unemployment continued to rise. At the same time, the process of deindustrialisation was underway and the UK economy experienced falling levels of employment in the energy and manufacturing sectors; unemployment reached 3 million in 1983 and continued to rise until 1985.

Despite the problem of unemployment, government policy was focused on inflation. In today's economic climate, where an annual rate of CPI rising above 4% and RPI of 5% is cause for concern, it is easy to forget that in May 1975 the RPI measure of inflation recorded a figure of 4.2% per month – an annual inflation rate of 24.2% for 1975 as a whole.

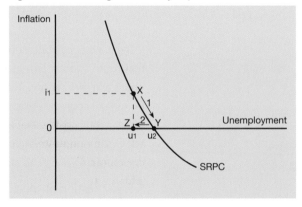

Figure 2.9: Reducing inflationary expectations

The impact of economic slowdown in the Monetarist model is shown in Figure 2.9.

As the economy moves along SRPC from point X to point Y there is higher unemployment and lower inflation in the short-run. The Monetarists argued that only by reducing inflationary expectations – breaking the wage-price spiral which fuels inflation – could households and firms regain a belief that prices and costs will be more stable. In the long-run, provided expectations are permanently shifted, the SRPC shifts inwards and the economy returns to the long-run equilibrium output and unemployment levels at point Z, with zero inflation.

Thus the opposite of stagflation – falling inflation and falling unemployment – is possible, but only through what may be a painful adjustment of consumer and business expectations. Chapter 3 will explore other ways in which the 'holy grail' of economists – low-inflationary growth – can be achieved.

Types of unemployment

Both the Keynesian and Monetarist models agree that even in a stable economy there may be some unemployment. For the economists this may be due to a degree of demand-deficiency, perhaps because the government is controlling aggregate demand to control inflation, but also due to frictional and structural factors.

Frictional unemployment is also called **search unemployment**, and arises when workers are between jobs. Frictional unemployment will always exist in an active labour market as redundancies occur, people take career breaks to travel or have a family, and as students leave education and try to enter the workforce. It may be the case that frictional unemployment will rise if economic growth is lower: the fewer job opportunities available, the longer it takes for workers to find a job at an acceptable wage.

Structural unemployment, on the other hand, presents a longer-term problem. This occurs when there is a mismatch between skills and vacancies; the labour market is creating jobs but they are not suitable for the workers who have seen their jobs disappear. Structural unemployment is a major problem in periods of deindustrialisation or when there is a major shift in the global pattern of production and demand.

Monetarists also stress the phenomenon of **real wage** or **classical unemployment**. The main difference between the Classical model (and its updated version, Monetarism) and the Keynesian model is the degree to which wages will adjust to soak up excess demand or supply of labour. In the case of recession, if wages are suitably flexible they should fall as the unemployed bid down the wages of the employed: microeconomic theory tells us that wherever there is excess supply for a good, price will fall. Thus unemployment effectively cures itself by forcing down the wages of all workers and increasing the employability of labour. Similarly, when demand is high and the economy is booming, this will create a labour shortage and drive wages upwards. Therefore any worker who remains without a job in the long-run is choosing to not work at the prevailing wage rate and is therefore voluntarily unemployed.

Keynes disagreed with this analysis. He proposed that labour markets did not work this simply and the 'downwards stickiness' of wages led to involuntary unemployment which could persist in the long-run.

The level of unemployment at U1 on both Figures 2.10 and 2.11 is called the **natural rate of unemployment** (NRU) or the **non-accelerating inflation rate of unemployment** (NAIRU).

There are various technical differences between these two measures, but at this level it is satisfactory to attribute the unemploy-

Figure 2.10: NAIRU – Monetarist view

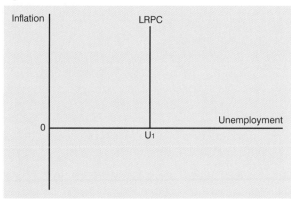

Figure 2.11: NAIRU – Keynesian view

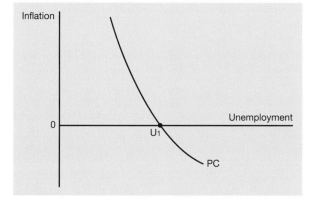

ment at both points to a combination of frictional, structural and real wage factors. The degree to which labour markets fail to clear, in either the short-run or long-run, therefore determines the natural rate of unemployment.

Types of inflation

Figure 2.12: Cost-push inflation

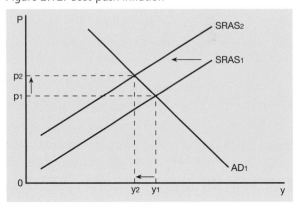

The causes of inflation can be divided into two types: cost-push and demand-pull. These are illustrated in Figures 2.12 and 2.13.

Inflation is a sustained increase in the general level of prices and this is measured using a price index. This index reflects the cost of living in the economy: the total prices of necessity goods (fuel, housing, food and clothing) and luxuries (e.g. cars, books about economics, music and holidays). These prices are weighted to produce a typical 'basket of goods' and in the UK are collected via the Family Expenditure Survey. RPI (Retail Price Index) and CPI (Consumer Price Index) monitor the total price of a 'basket of goods' over time; this basket reflects the typical expenditure of an average household. The basket is updated to reflect changes in tastes and the CPI is particularly sophisticated in the way it makes substitution decisions where the price of one good has risen or fallen. For example, if the price of air travel rises the weight used for flights will fall slightly and a substitute, such as rail travel, will see a slight rise in its weighting.

Figure 2.13: Demand-pull inflation

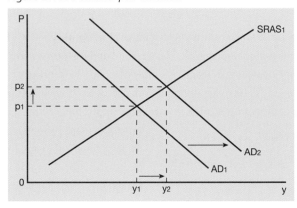

Price deflation arises when the basket of goods falls in total price. Falling prices in individual markets is not uncommon: in the UK in recent years the prices of goods such as electrical appliances and cars have fallen due to greater competition and the influx of cheap imports from newly-industrialising countries such as China. This should not be confused with another meaning of this word. This second meaning refers to the situation when the total spending of the average household declines. Even if all prices are falling in the economy, if household income is rising the typical basket of goods will expand and total spending will rise. On the other hand, if incomes are falling to such an extent that households are actually spending less on a month-by-month basis this deflationary effect can be interpreted as a very worrying sign in the economy and associated with rapid economic downturn and recession.

Figure 2.14: Benign ('good') deflation

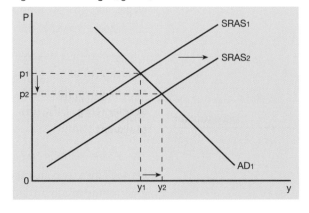

Deflation can therefore be seen as either benign (higher supply due to competition or technological breakthrough leading to falling prices and higher output levels – see Figure 2.14) or malign (falling demand due to falling

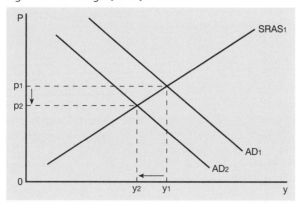

Figure 2.15: Malign ('bad') deflation

incomes and confidence leading to falling prices and lower output levels – see Figure 2.15).

The role of expectations is important in determining the degree of inflationary pressure in the economy. In the 1970s when inflation was very high, workers reacted to increases in the cost of living by demanding high wage increases to attempt to maintain (at the minimum) constant real incomes. This increased the costs of employers and prices rose as firms tried to pass some of these higher costs onto consumers. Thus demand-pull and cost-push factors combined to create a **wage-price spiral**. Figure 2.9 earlier in the chapter shows the deflationary policies necessary in such circumstances to bring such extreme levels of inflation under control.

Summary questions

1. What does the conventional Phillips curve show?

2. To what extent does stagflation appear to break down the Phillips curve relationship?

3. What insight does the Phillips curve offer in terms of designing suitable policy responses to problems in the macroeconomy? Should different types of inflation and unemployment be treated differently?

4. What are the weaknesses and dangers of using a price index to model inflationary experiences in the economy? Why may different groups (such as pensioners, students) be vulnerable to microeconomic changes which may be averaged out for the economy as a whole?

5. Distinguish between 'good' deflation and 'bad' deflation. How would we know which type of deflation the economy is experiencing?

Extension questions

A. Why may the Classical school of thought have believed that wages could adjust perfectly in the long-run? Could this be linked to the nature of the UK and other European economies in the 18th and 19th Centuries?

B. In light of your answer to Question 1 above, how might the attempts of the Monetarist economists in the UK and USA be linked to the assumptions made by Classical economists before the 1930s?

C. The rational expectations school can be seen as an adaption and extension of Monetarist theory. This model proposes that any increase in AD, or the money supply, will only create inflation and there will be no increase in real output or fall in unemployment – even in the short-run. Find out more about the rational expectations model and see how their ideas fit into the ideas discussed in this chapter.

Chapter 3

Growth and Productivity

Aggregate demand and aggregate supply

The conventional view of the macroeconomy is of two competing influences: the interplay between the demand side and the supply side. GDP can rise or fall – and inflation and unemployment can both result – according to changes in AD or LRAS. The models shown in Chapter 2 provide the tools for analysing the side effects of changes in aggregate demand.

The economic cycle makes achieving all macroeconomic objectives simultaneously very difficult. In a recession, inflation is usually low (unless there is stagflation) and the current account may improve as demand for imports declines in line with the demand for all goods and services, but unemployment is usually high and the government's finances may come under strain as the fiscal drag effect of lower tax revenue and higher government spending pushes the budget into deficit. In a boom, unemployment and the budget position should improve, but inflation and the current account become more problematic as higher spending puts upward pressure on prices (and possibly therefore costs) and the economy sucks in imports to meet the high levels of demand. Throughout the economic cycle, it is this volatility in economic growth which leads to the 'boom and bust' associated with periods of fluctuating growth.

Supply-side growth and macroeconomic policy objectives

Figure 3.1 Non-inflationary growth

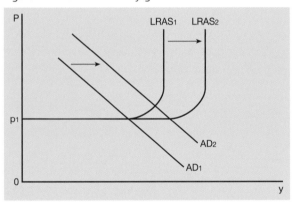

Supply-side growth offers the possibility of steady, sustainable growth and job creation in a non-inflationary environment, possibly even alongside improvement in the current account of the balance of payments. Thus even when aggregate demand is rising, expansion in the productive capacity of the economy can keep inflation and current account problems under control as shown in Figure 3.1. Supply-side growth occurs when the quantity and/or quality of factors of production (land, labour, capital and enterprise) increase, i.e. when productivity rises. Figure 3.2 shows the impact of an increase in the long-run productive potential of the economy.

Figure 3.2 Increased productive potential

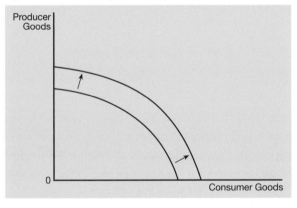

It is useful to distinguish between supply side growth (which may occur naturally, e.g. through increases in population due to net immigration or rising life expectancy) and supply side policy (which specifically targets factors such as labour participation rates or the education and skills of the workforce).

Supply-side policy has both microeconomic and macroeconomic impacts. Changes in taxation, privatisation and labour market reform can help to boost the efficiency of factors of production, but they will also have direct impacts on the specific markets concerned. For example, privatisation of the telecommunications industry in the UK has opened the market to greater competition, lowering costs and improving consumer choice and increasing consumer surplus in the process. This has, in addition, helped to lower business costs, thus raising productivity (however slightly) across the whole economy.

Demand management and supply-side policy in the UK

Although the Keynesian and Monetarist schools disagree on the exact effectiveness of demand-management policies in the short-run and long-run, UK governments since 1997 under 'New Labour' have built on both models to pursue an economic regime which has stressed the importance of both the supply-side (in driving economic growth – trend growth – onwards) and the demand-side (providing macroeconomic stability around the trend rate of growth). This can be summarised as an attempt to control the fluctuations associated with the economic cycle whilst targeting factor productivity (output per input) across the economy.

Table 3.1: Growth, inflation and unemployment: demand and supply factors

	GDP	Inflation	Unemployment
Demand-side	Economic upturn and downturn	Demand-pull inflation	Demand-deficient unemployment
Supply-side	Economic growth	Cost-push inflation	Structural unemployment

The Misery Index

Figure 3.3: The Misery Index (CPI + Claimant Count) %

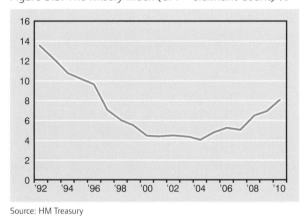

Source: HM Treasury

The twin problems of inflation and unemployment can be encapsulated in the Misery Index, first proposed by the economist Arthur Okun. The idea is simple: adding the rate of inflation to the rate of unemployment gives a rapid assessment of the stability of an economy at a point in time.

Figure 3.3 shows the Misery Index for the UK in recent years. Since its peak in 1992 the index declined steadily until 2005 and then inflationary pressure and a slowing labour market pushed the index upwards.

Supply-side policy since 1997

The strength of the UK economy since 1997 undoubtedly helped the New Labour government to re-election in 2001 and 2005. No Labour government in the UK had previously completed two full consecutive terms in office and the 'prudent and cautious' approach to fiscal and monetary policy helped to reassure the public, business and the City that a Labour government could deliver economic growth without high inflation.

How was this done? We can identify several key factors behind the New Labour 'economic miracle' as follows:

Higher spending on the NHS and education

A healthier and more highly skilled workforce can produce higher quantity and quality goods and services. Gains in productivity are fundamental to supply-side growth. Data on UK productivity is shown in Figure 3.7.

Benefits of earlier reforms

The 1980s was a period of painful modernisation for the UK. Trade union power was reduced by legislative measures and the UK experienced considerable deindustrialisation, changing from a major employer in manufacturing to a knowledge-based, tertiary economy which specialises in producing and exporting financial services and cultural and intellectual output such as media goods (music, TV, film) and education. In addition, the 'Big Bang' deregulation of the financial sector in 1986 and the privatisation of key industries such as telecommunications and transport (if not always with total success) have made the business environment more competitive and innovative. This has also resulted in greater flexibility in labour and capital markets and allowed firms to employ the right people and find the right funding to do business successfully.

Falling inflationary expectations

When consumers and firms expect prices to rise significantly, they may behave in ways which make this more likely to happen. Similarly, expectations of a low inflation economy tend to be self-fulfilling. The act of granting independence to the Bank of England in 1997, with a clear remit to control inflation within a defined target range, helped to maintain an economic environment in which inflation remained under control – and just as importantly, was expected to remain under control.

Globalisation

This will be discussed further in Chapter 6. Meantime we can refer to the influx of cheap imported goods which has helped to keep consumer prices low (reducing demand-pull inflationary pressures). Another aspect of globalisation has been the influx of foreign workers willing to work hard for relatively low wages which has allowed firms and households to benefit from lower factor prices (alleviating cost-push inflation).

Stable aggregate demand

Monetary policy was placed in the hands of the independent Monetary Policy Committee of the Bank of England in 1997 (one of the first acts of the new government), and fiscal policy has been constrained by clear rules; this has helped firms and households to enjoy low inflation and steady growth. Consumer and business confidence grew throughout the 1990s, fuelling greater spending by households and firms, providing greater tax revenue for the government to use to spend on public services (see the first factor mentioned above).

Weak sterling after 1992

When sterling crashed spectacularly out of the Exchange Rate Mechanism (the pound was tied to the deutschmark in a precursor to adopting the Euro) there were widespread fears that the UK would suffer a permanent loss of economic strength relative to the other major European economies. But the devaluation of sterling improved the competitiveness of UK-produced goods and services, both at home and in international markets. Figure 1.2 in Chapter 1 shows just how well the UK grew in real terms after leaving the ERM.

Some criticisms of New Labour supply-side policy

Criticism of the governments of Blair and Brown regarding supply-side policies include:

Low 'value for money' in public services

Despite large increases in funding, some economists argue that the NHS and education systems are still not effective and efficient in improving social welfare.

Figure 3.4: The National Minimum Wage

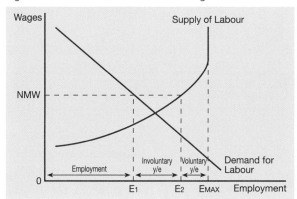

Increased 'red tape'

Bureaucracy under New Labour arguably became more complex, adding to the costs of firms in monitoring and maintaining (for example) health and safety legislation.

The National Minimum Wage

Supply-side policy is usually associated with reducing or removing labour market imperfections. The National Minimum Wage (NMW), a flagship policy introduced in 1998, was expected to increase involuntary unemployment (people willing to work at the prevailing wage rate but unable to find a job – see Figure 3.4). This may be due to efficiency drives in the sectors involved and perhaps the replacement of people with machines, where possible, to avoid the higher labour costs. However, despite fears about the impact of NMW on employment and unemployment levels (particularly in the lowest paid jobs and sectors) Figure 3.5 shows that, when compared with previous data, jobs for the UK workforce remained reasonably stable. Of course, it could be argued that the

Figure 3.5: UK unemployment (Labour Force Survey and Claimant Count, millions, seasonally adjusted)

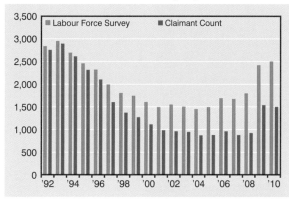

Source: ONS

microeconomic impact of unemployment in certain sectors was masked by benign macroeconomic conditions which kept job creation strong as the macroeconomy grew quickly. Alternatively, perhaps the NMW is at a sufficiently low level to neither increase the incentive to work for low-skilled workers, nor reduce the incentive of employing them.

Figure 3.6: House prices and stock market indices 1990-2010 (% change)

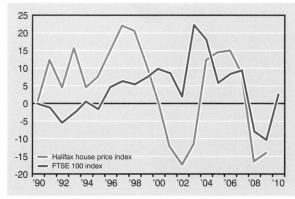

Source: HM Treasury

Rising tax levels

Increases in the tax burden (the percentage of income paid in taxes) may arise during periods of strong economic growth as more households are drawn into higher income tax brackets. In addition, rising house and asset prices may increase the levels of stamp duty and capital gains tax paid to the government. Tax Freedom Day is the (theoretical) point in the year when the average household stops working for the government and starts working for themselves (see Table 3.2). There

Table 3.2: Tax Freedom Day

Year	Tax Freedom Day
2002	May 27
2003	May 25
2004	May 28
2005	May 30
2006	June 4
2007	June 1
2008	May 30
2009	May 24
2010	May 27
2011	May 30

For comparison (selected years):

Year	Tax Freedom Day
1992	28 May
1982	15 June
1972	12 May
1964	24th April

Figure 3.7: UK productivity growth (% p.a.)

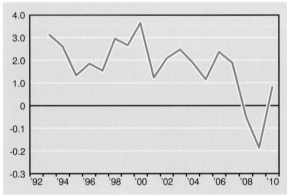

Source: HM Treasury

has been widespread criticism of the 'stealth taxes' introduced by New Labour, but data on increases in house prices and (ever more volatile) in the stock market (see Figure 3.6) may help to explain why the tax burden has risen over the period shown. It is interesting to note the high tax burden for the UK in the 1980s despite this period being associated with low taxation and free market policies.

The productivity story: UK and other countries

Data on productivity can be complicated by other economic variables. For example, during a period of economic slowdown it is not unusual to see productivity rise, and in upturn and boom for productivity growth to slow. This is related to the suitability of factors of production, particularly labour. As the pool of available workers declines, firms may have to recruit less able – or at least, less relevantly skilled – workers to fill vacancies. On the other hand, firms cutting workforce levels as a result of falling demand will tend to make less productive workers redundant first. This is certainly supported by the surge in productivity growth in 2010 as the economy emerged from recession, although in both 2008 and 2009 productivity growth was negative.

Bureaucracy under New Labour arguably became more complex.

Table 3.3: Comparative productivity growth (% change per year) for G7 countries

	Germany	USA	Japan	UK	Canada	France	Italy
1995	4.8	0.4	4.3	1.3	1.3	1.7	7.3
1996	3.5	2.6	3.2	1.9	-0.2	0.9	-0.6
1997	6.9	1.5	5.5	1.6	2.6	0.9	4.2
1998	4.2	2.9	-3.0	3.0	2.4	1.2	0.3
1999	1.6	3.3	3.6	2.7	3.3	2.0	1.7
2000	6.0	3.3	6.9	3.7	3.5	0.9	3.8
2001	0.1	3.0	-2.9	1.3	1.1	0.9	-2.1
2002	1.7	4.5	3.8	2.1	1.4	-0.4	-2.1
2003	2.8	3.6	4.9	2.5	0.2	1.7	-2.0
2004	5.1	2.8	4.9	1.9	0.2	2.2	1.1
2005	5.3	1.6	2.2	1.2	2.4	1.4	0.1
2006	6.7	0.9	3.2	2.4	1.1	1.2	0.3
2007	5.2	1.6	2.4	1.9	0.0	0.9	0.1
2008	-2.0	1.0	-3.0	-0.5	-0.9	0.8	-0.2
2009	-14.9	3.7	-15.1	-1.8	0.4	0.8	-0.8
2010	14.4	3.8	11.7	0.8	1.4	0.4	-1.1
16 year average	**3.2**	**2.5**	**2.0**	**1.6**	**1.3**	**1.1**	**0.6**

Source: Bank of England

Supply-side policy since 2010

The Coalition government which formed in May 2010 has proposed and begun to implement a policy of fiscal austerity, combined with plans to boost incentives in the private sector.

Fiscal austerity, by gradually reducing the size of the budget deficit and (eventually) reducing national debt, will in theory lead to lower interest payments on government debt, freeing up funds for spending in other areas (see Figure 3.8).

Other supply-side policies proposed by the Coalition government include:
- ▶ Possible reductions in immigration into the UK from outside the European Union.
- ▶ Reductions in bureaucracy for firms, e.g. health and safety legislation.
- ▶ Changes to some welfare payments, e.g. caps on housing benefit payments.

With respect to immigration, the advantages and disadvantages of free trade and open labour markets are discussed in greater detail in Chapters 5, 6 and 7.

Figure 3.8: UK Government spending by category 2010-2011 (£bn)

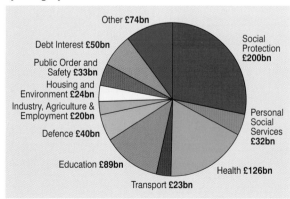

Source: Office for Budget Responsibility 2011-2012 estimates.

Some policies on education already put in place as of 2011 could be seen to be detrimental to long-term growth, such as:
- ▶ Increases in maximum university tuition fees.
- ▶ Abolishing the Education Maintenance Allowance for school pupils aged 16-18.

By reducing the attractiveness of education, these policies could be argued to seriously restrict future productivity growth in the UK and a loss of competitive advantage against other countries.

The Laffer Curve and crowding out

Fiscal policy is usually associated with controlling actual output using taxes and spending to influence the level of aggregate demand in the economy. However, taxes and spending can also influence the supply-side of the economy.

Figure 3.9: Laffer Curve

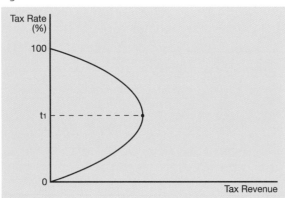

Government spending on healthcare and education has already been discussed, but research and development can also increase the long-run growth potential of the economy by increasing efficiency through new technologies and more sophisticated management techniques. This can also be aided by a favourable tax regime which allows entrepreneurs to enjoy a higher proportion of their profits as a reward for successful innovation.

The impact of tax rates on the macroeconomy can be explored using the Laffer Curve, which relates the rate of taxation in the economy (the percentage of tax to income paid by households, or the percentage of tax to profit paid by entrepreneurs) to the tax revenue (the total tax yield received by the government from taxpayers). It is assumed that tax revenue will be zero at two points: where the tax rate is zero (i.e. the government collects nothing of the incomes and/or profits available), and where it is 100% (it is assumed that no one would work if all their income and/or profit was handed straight to the government).

The Laffer Curve suggests there is an optimal tax rate at which tax revenue is maximised. Note that a change in the tax rate will either increase or decrease tax revenue depending on whether the current rate is above or below t_1.

The Laffer Curve is often used to argue for tax cuts. Assuming the actual tax rate is initially above t_1, income or corporation tax rates can be reduced and the government will actually receive higher tax receipts because, it is argued, lower tax rates increase the incentive to work, and thus the higher level of employment outweighs the lower tax yield per worker.

This argument assumes that a higher supply of workers, incentivised by lower tax rates, will automatically increase the amount of work available. It is also assumes that an influx of workers will not reduce average wage rates (as might be anticipated by a microeconomic analysis of the labour market).

The Laffer Curve can also be used to justify either higher or lower tax rates, particularly if a higher level of tax revenue is deemed desirable, for example where increasing equality and providing high quality public and merit goods is the objective. Depending on the starting point (above or below t_1) this will be achieved by either a tax rate increase or decrease.

Figure 3.10: An alternative Laffer Curve

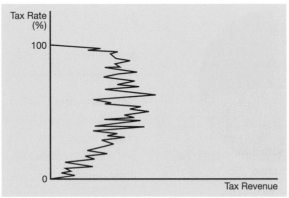

Critics of the Laffer Curve argue that it lacks empirical basis (it was allegedly first drawn over lunch on a napkin by Arthur Laffer) and that it assumes the relationship between tax rates and revenue has only one maximum point, or is unimodal; in reality, the distribution of tax revenue versus tax rate may be multi-modal. An example is shown in Figure 3.10 (which also it has to be said readily lacks empirical evidence).

The impact of tax rates on the reporting and monitoring of taxable income might also be considered. It may be the case that at higher rates of tax there may be greater tax evasion (which is the illegal non-payment of tax when it should be paid) and tax avoidance (which is the legal process of managing one's finances to avoid paying tax, perhaps through tax loopholes or trusts). In addition, high rates of tax in comparison with other countries are likely to lead to net emigration of both workers (and perhaps the most highly skilled workers, creating a 'brain drain') and jobs (as multinational companies move headquarters to countries with more favourable tax regimes).

The advantages of long run growth

Supply-side or long-run growth can neutralise the inflationary pressures which may result from higher aggregate demand, as we saw earlier in Figure 3.1. This explains why, over time, the level of economic activity can increase alongside the real standard of living. When compared with twenty, ten or five years ago, most households in the UK enjoy cheaper and higher quality goods; this has resulted from supply-side growth in the UK (rising UK productivity reduces the average cost of production) as well as the power of globalisation to increase world productivity rates.

Figure 3.11: Imports and the PPF

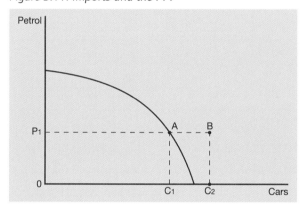

In addition, higher aggregate supply will not worsen the current account position in the same way as higher aggregate demand.

Figure 3.11 shows an economy operating outside the Production Possibility Frontier (PPF). Domestic factors of production are fully utilised at point A and further consumption of cars is only possible (without reducing petrol consumption) by importing ($C_2 - C_1$) cars from abroad. This suggests a current account deficit and, in the long-run, will be unsustainable without significant outflows of currency and gold reserves.

Figure 3.12: Economic growth and trade

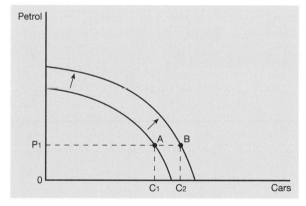

Figure 3.12 shows how output point B becomes sustainable in the long-run through economic growth, allowing C_2 cars and P_1 petrol to be produced domestically and thus without the need for imports.

Thus long-run growth creates jobs and output without putting pressure on other objectives such as low inflation and a satisfactory position on the current account.

Other key advantages of long-run economic growth include:

Rising material standard of living
Households and firms enjoy better levels of nutrition and comfort and a wider range of goods and services.

Fiscal dividend
Higher tax revenues can be used to fund better healthcare to increase life expectancy and the quality of life; higher spending on education can also increase human capital and cultural enrichment; establishment of a welfare state can reduce social exclusion.

Better goods and services

Technology can improve the reliability and longevity of goods and services in both the public and private sector; contestability, competition and innovation can create dynamic markets where goods and services increasingly cater to the specific wants and needs of consumers.

The disadvantages of long run growth

The unconditional benefit of higher levels of economic activity is not universally accepted. Economists have identified several possible disadvantages of economic growth:

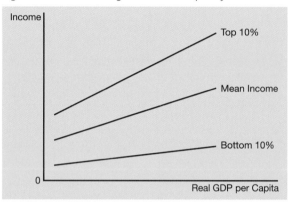

Figure 3.13: Economic growth and inequality

Impacts on inequality

Economic growth may be associated with rising inequality. As economies become more specialised, it is those workers with scarcer skills who become more highly valued. This relationship is shown in Figure 3.13 where the earnings of the top 10th percentile and bottom 10th percentile diverge as average earnings (the 50th percentile) rise.

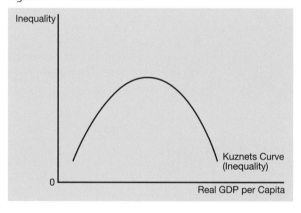

Figure 3.14: Kuznets Curve

Inequality may bring social conflict and exclusion, which in turn leads to problems such as long-run unemployment and crime which carry serious economic costs on both a local and national level. This perceived link between greater economic activity and inequality was suggested long ago in 1955 by Simon Kuznets. He suggested that greater inequality may result in the short-run as an economy develops, but in the long-run this might become less true as skills gaps close (lower paid workers identify shortages in higher paid work, and retrain; thus shortages even out) and institutions such as the welfare state and universal education emerge and become more stable. This proposition is a contentious one but we can at least state that economic growth alone may not lead to a narrowing in income differentials.

The distinction between economic growth and economic development is important and will be covered in Chapter 9.

Environmental degradation and depletion

Economic activity uses resources, some of which may be scarce, such as fossil fuels. This criticism of the growth of modern economies is closely associated with the Green Movement, but fear over the impact of industrialisation and urbanisation dates back to the Industrial Revolution in Britain and the rise of the Romantic movement who argued that the spread of towns and cities and the rise of manufacturing was destroying an idyllic, rural way of life.

Economists have also proposed the existence of an environmental Kuznets curve, which allows for greater levels of pollution and fossil fuel use in the short-run but argues that in the long-run increasing levels of wealth and environmental awareness will encourage and allow substantial investment in cleaner technologies. Alternatively, economies entering the post-industrial phase of development will import more energy, raw materials and manufactured goods from newly-industrialising countries, thus shifting local environmental issues into the developing world; this process is known as 'environmental dumping'.

'Affluenza'

Perhaps well-off people in rich economies do not know how lucky they are... This phenomenon of Affluenza has attracted much media attention in the consideration of the importance of absolute versus relative poverty in determining happiness and quality of life. **Absolute Poverty** arises when an individual's daily income falls below an agreed minimum level (for example, the World Bank measure of US$1 per day). In economies such as those in Europe or North America, even after adjusting for relative prices and access to public services, absolute poverty is very rare and will be restricted to those who are homeless and on the very fringes of society. **Relative Poverty**, on the other hand, refers to an individual's position in society in relation to others. Thus a teenager whose trainers are unfashionable or whose MP3 player does not hold as much music as their friends' may feel 'poor' in comparison, even though access to food, sanitation, clean water, healthcare, shelter, warm clothing and a quality education is plentiful (of these measures listed, lack of access to any two or more is regarded as absolute poverty by the United Nations).

'Affluenza' highlights the impact of a consumer society on individuals, groups and communities by arguing that long working hours, the blurring of leisure and work activities and the decline of family life and traditional social interaction have diminished our happiness and made us poorer in the process. Critics of the affluenza argument might argue that effective social policies can be used to redistribute income where possible – and also that, given the choice, they would choose relative over absolute poverty every time!

Figure 3.15: Lorenz Curves

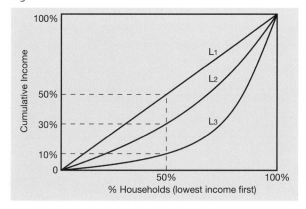

The Gini coefficient and the Lorenz curve measure income (in)equality. The Gini coefficient is a ratio with a value between 0 and 1. The closer the Gini is to 0, the more equal the distribution. This can also be illustrated using a Lorenz curve, as in Figure 3.15.

L1 shows the line of perfect equality. For example, 50% of households enjoys 50% of income. L2 shows greater inequality than L1: the poorest half of the population only enjoys 30% of income. L3 shows greater inequality still: the poorest half of the population only enjoys 10% of income. The Gini coefficient will therefore be highest for L3 and lowest (0) for L1.

Inequality and economic growth: the debate

It has been assumed above that the cause and effect between greater inequality and higher economic growth is that the latter causes the former. It may be the case, however, that the opposite is true and that inequality is an important determinant of growth by driving people and entrepreneurs to work harder to escape poverty. The fear of social exclusion, it is argued, therefore increases productivity as the lack of a safety net such as a welfare state (providing benefits and free education and healthcare to those who would otherwise go without them) reinforces the need for high levels of participation in the labour market. However, the counter argument may be that a lack of earning potential in the formal economy may result in greater crime as earnings have to be derived from the shadow or informal economy. In addition, there will always be vulnerable individuals and groups who require help and financial support as their earning potential is very low.

It would appear, therefore, that some degree of inequality is inevitable in any market economy, but the degree to which this should be reduced will depend on how important it is perceived to be in increasing economic growth (through increasing incentives to avoid personal poverty) and reducing economic growth (through reducing the mobility of labour and incurring costs on society through unemployment and crime).

Summary questions

1. What are the possible weaknesses of using a Misery Index to determine economic policy?

2. To what extent has supply-side policy been successful in the UK in recent years? What are the main factors determining this?

3. Explain one benefit and one cost of rising tax levels for the economy.

4. How does UK productivity compare with other G7 members? Why may this be the case?

5. Is economic growth (in the long-run sense) a good thing? If so, what can be done to limit the damage it may cause? If not, why is it apparently important to individuals and governments?

Extension questions

A. Research data on the UK economy in the 1970s and 1980s. Use this to compile a Misery Index and compare this to Figure 3.3 in this chapter.

B. How useful is Tax Freedom Day as a measure of economic welfare? Research Tax Freedom Day in other countries and consider why this measure differs between them.

C. What are the likely implications for UK productivity of current government policies?

Chapter 4

Exchange Rates and Exchange Rate Systems

Exchange rates and the FOREX market

An exchange rate is the price of one currency in terms of another currency; for example, £1 = $2. A movement in the exchange rate therefore affects both currencies and if, say, £1 = $2.10 after the change, sterling is said to have strengthened and the dollar to have weakened.

Since 1992, the UK has operated a floating exchange rate whereby the value of sterling in terms of other currencies has been allowed to fluctuate according to market forces. The market in this case is the foreign exchange or FOREX market. The main influences on the demand and supply of sterling are trade, investment and speculation.

Figure 4.1: The Foreign Exchange market

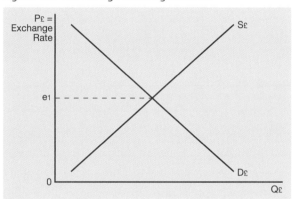

The currency will strengthen or appreciate if there is an increase in the demand for UK exports (the demand for a currency is a *derived demand*, related to international trade), if UK interest rates rise relative to other countries' rates (attracting inflows of investment, known as *hot money inflows*) or if speculators believe the value of the currency will rise (thereby offering the chance of short-run profits to take advantage of the price movement).

Similarly, the currency will weaken or depreciate if there is an increase in imports into the UK (necessitating the purchase of foreign currencies with sterling), if UK interest rates fall relative to other countries' (creating hot money outflows), or if speculators believe the value of the currency will fall.

Floating exchange rates are not the only option. Sometimes governments choose to target a particular exchange rate (usually 'pegging' to a strong currency) and use measures to maintain that level in the FOREX market.

Figure 4.2: A target exchange rate

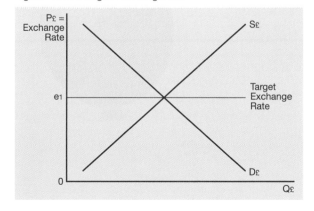

Figure 4.2 shows the target exchange rate e_1. A change in the demand or supply of sterling will move the equilibrium price of sterling away from e_1, and in this instance the government and/or the central bank will intervene to counter such a movement.

Figure 4.3 shows a situation where there has been a rise in the value of sterling due to higher demand reflected in the shift of demand from $D_{£1}$ to $D_{£2}$. This could arise due to increased demand for UK goods abroad, higher relative interest rates (this could happen if, for example, there are significant interest rate cuts in other economies) or if speculators believe sterling will rise. The government or central bank can act to reduce demand or increase supply of sterling. The options are thus as follows:

Figure 4.3: Upward pressure on a fixed exchange rate

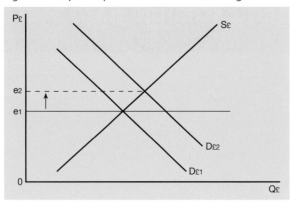

1. Either cutting interest rates, thereby creating hot money outflows and reducing demand for sterling; or

2. Selling sterling and buying foreign currencies. These are known as open market operations in the FOREX market.

September 1992 was the last time the UK operated a fixed exchange rate system. Sterling was pegged to the Deutschmark (the German currency pre-Euro) as part of the ERM (Exchange Rate Mechanism, a precursor to Eurozone membership) but by 16th September the currency was struggling to maintain its value despite intensive and drastic government intervention (aggressive buying of sterling using reserves of gold and foreign currencies and an increase in the base rate from 10% to 12% in the morning, followed by a promise to raise base rate to 15% in the afternoon). Speculators continued to sell sterling, convinced it could not stay at the target ERM rate, and eventually the government conceded defeat in an episode known as 'Black Wednesday.'

The case for floating exchange rates

The main advantage of a floating exchange rate regime is the lack of opportunities for speculative attack – this may appear particularly attractive given events such as Black Wednesday discussed above.

In addition, the absence of government intervention frees policy instruments such as the base rate to pursue other objectives such as low inflation. An independent Bank of England would have been severely restricted in achieving its successful targeting of inflation if every base rate adjustment had to be considered in the context of its impact on the exchange rate target as well.

The main advantage of floating exchange rates is a lower risk of speculative attack.

Arguably, the main advantage of a floating rate is the opportunity for *automatic adjustment* on the balance of payments. In theory, if the demand for imports outstrips the demand for exports (as is the case in the UK at present) the exchange rate should fall, reducing the price of UK goods abroad and increasing import prices. This should lead to improvement in the current account (see later in the chapter for a more detailed analysis).

The case for fixed exchange rates

Fixed exchange rates offer stability. Providing the target can be sustained, consumers and firms in both (or all, if more than one economy is pegged to a particular currency) countries benefit from the knowledge that the prices of internationally traded goods and services will remain comparable at a constant rate. In addition, returns on overseas investment and incomes from abroad can be converted, over time, at a constant rate and this certainty creates stability and increases trade and investment within the fixed rate area.

There may be dynamic gains from such stability. Greater specialisation may arise, resulting in economies of scale and a deepening of economic integration. This reduces average costs, and therefore hopefully prices, over time and leads to greater efficiency in the long-run. It may also be argued that a fixed exchange rate imposes economic discipline on governments and central banks. Expansionary policy would result in the economy 'sucking in imports' and thus push the current account into crisis and put downward pressure on the currency.

The Sterling exchange rate for the Dollar and Euro

Figure 4.4: Sterling-US Dollar exchange rate (yearly average) $ per £

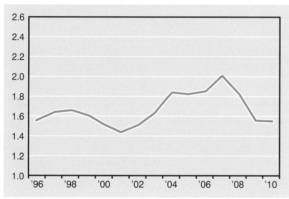

Source: Bank of England

Figure 4.5: Sterling-Euro exchange rate (yearly average) € per £

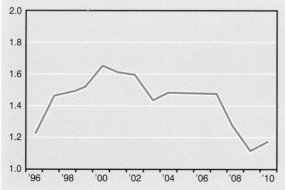

Source: Bank of England

Figure 4.4 shows how sterling has fluctuated against the dollar over the past 15 years. From 2001 sterling appreciated against the dollar until the recession from 2008-09 when it weakened significantly. This depreciation is mirrored in Figure 4.5 which shows sterling weakening against the euro in the same period. Economists estimate the impact of this depreciation in sterling added 1% to GDP over this period (in effect, limiting the severity of the recession by 1%).

Changes in exchange rates influence the economy in two key ways: by changing the price of UK exports in foreign markets, and the price of imported goods in the UK.

These impacts are shown in Table 4.1.

Depreciation, Appreciation, Devaluation and Revaluation

Changes in the exchange rate have different names, depending on whether the exchange rate is fixed or floating.

Table 4.1

	Stronger Currency	**Weaker Currency**
Fixed Exchange Rate	Revaluation	Devaluation
Floating Exchange Rate	Appreciation	Depreciation
Price of UK exports	↑	↓
Price of imports into UK	↓	↑

Depreciation and the current account (J-curve)

A weakening of the domestic currency is expected, in the long-run, to improve the current account position as the price of domestically-produced goods fall in international markets (thus boosting exports) and the prices of imported foreign goods rise (thus reducing imports). However, a closer examination – using price elasticity of demand – is required.

The value of exports (X) refers to the average price of exports multiplied by the quantity, or volume, of exports. The value of imports (M) refers to the average price of imports multiplied by the quantity, or volume, of imports.

Price elasticity of demand measures the responsiveness of demand to a change in price, and for the current account position (X-M) to improve in the long-run the sum of the elasticities for exports and imports must exceed one. This is known as the **Marshall-Lerner condition** and written as

$PED_X + PED_M > 1$

where PED_X is the price elasticity of demand for exports and PED_M is the price elasticity of demand for imports.

Price elasticity generally increases over time, thus in the long-run the Marshall-Lerner condition is generally satisfied. However, in the short-run the responsiveness of exports and imports to changes in their prices may be much lower.

Figure 4.6: The J-Curve

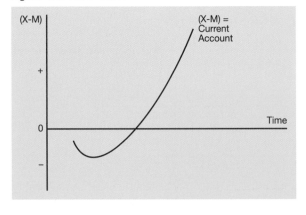

Figure 4.6 shows how a depreciation in the currency may, in the short-run, actually worsen the position on the current account. When the currency weakens the price of domestically-produced goods falls abroad. This should increase demand, but in the short-run foreign purchasers may be tied into contracts and agreements and until they can change their suppliers to take account of shifts in the relative price of UK goods demand may not increase significantly. There may also be an information lag if the change in price is not immediately obvious to all economic agents and, in addition, the price received by UK exporters does not change even though the price in the importing country does change. Thus the value of exports (X) will rise, but perhaps not to a great extent.

The price of imported goods will rise when the domestic currency weakens. However, UK purchasers may be tied into agreements and contracts or may simply not realise that import prices are rising relative to domestic prices. It is possible, if the price elasticity of demand for imports is very low, that rising prices actually increase the value of imports (M) in the short-run if prices increase by a higher proportion than the volume of imports falls.

This short-run elasticity explains the initial worsening of the current account position after depreciation. This may be particularly noticeable in an economy such as the UK which has a high propensity to import (in particular) manufactured goods. The marginal propensity to import is the ratio of additional imports to additional income. In a boom, therefore, imports rise rapidly in the UK (see the recent experience on the current account) and even with a weakening pound it may take time for the competitiveness of UK goods to improve enough to actually see an improvement in the balance of (X-M).

Figure 4.6 assumes the Marshall-Lerner condition is satisfied and thus the current account improves in the long-run and the initial downturn is reversed in the long-run. This fall, followed by a rise, characterises the J-Curve.

Appreciation and the current account (Reverse J-Curve)

Figure 4.7: The Reverse J-Curve

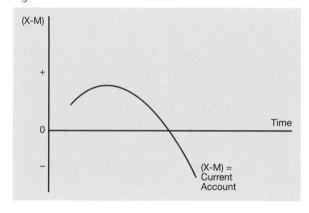

A stronger domestic currency should, in the long-run, lead to a worsening of the position on the current account. However, in the short-run changes in demand may lag behind changes in price and thus the current account may actually improve as the price of imports fall and thus M declines before the lower prices trigger higher demand. Again, the price of UK exports abroad will rise but this will not increase the unit price received by UK firms, but in the long-run there will be a fall in the demand for UK exports and a rise in the level of imports.

Thus in the long-run, providing the Marshall-Lerner condition is met, the current account position will worsen after a short-run improvement – hence the Reverse J-Curve shown in Figure 4.7.

The exchange rate as a policy instrument

The influence of the exchange rate on the current account balance (X-M), and therefore on aggregate demand [C + I + G + (X - M)], means that a change in the exchange rate can have an important effect on the performance of the macroeconomy. A weaker currency (either through deliberate devaluation in a fixed regime or as a side-effect of lower interest rates in a floating regime) will have – in the long-run – an inflationary or expansionary effect on the economy. A stronger currency (either through deliberate revaluation in a fixed regime or as a side-effect of higher interest rates in a floating regime) will have – in the long-run – a deflationary or contractionary effect on the economy.

At present in the UK the exchange rate of sterling against other currencies is allowed to float, and so the impact of the exchange rate is a secondary effect of changes in the Bank of England base rate. The base rate influences all interest rates in the economy, and interest rates and the exchange rates are positively linked.

An increase in the base rate will put upward pressure on all interest rates in the economy, in turn appreciating the currency. Higher interest rates reduce consumption and investment and the stronger currency reduces

Figure 4.8: The impact of a stronger domestic currency

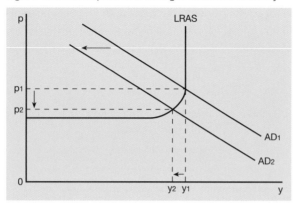

Figure 4.9: The impact of a weaker domestic currency

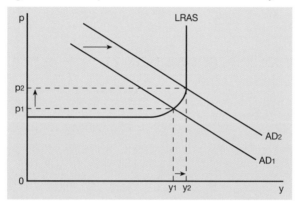

A weak currency can push up import prices.

exports and increases imports (assuming the Marshall-Lerner condition is met – see above). This worsening of the current account – a fall in the (X-M) component of aggregate demand, adds to the deflationary power of a higher base rate. As AD shifts back (see Figure 4.8) there is downward pressure on prices and, depending on the starting point, lower output and higher unemployment.

Similarly, a cut in the base rate will reduce interest rates and depreciate the currency as hot money outflows arise. This is due to global investors seeking higher rates of return in alternative currencies which now enjoy relatively higher interest rates.

The lower interest rates stimulate consumption and investment and the weaker currency boosts exports and reduces the attractiveness of imports, hence (X-M) rises and aggregate demand rises. Assuming the economy is in the trade-off section of the Long Run Aggregate Supply curve there will be an increase in output and prices and a fall in unemployment as shown on Figure 4.9.

It may be assumed, therefore, that a weaker currency is preferable to a stronger currency whenever output and jobs can be increased without excessive fears about inflation. However, there are advantages of a strong currency. For example, the UK has a high marginal propensity to import, particularly in goods, and a strong pound keeps the price of these imports lower. This can help to alleviate inflationary pressure in the economy, albeit at the expense of a large current account deficit. This is sometimes referred to as **imported deflation**. Other economies, too, may prefer a stronger currency if they rely on imports such as energy or raw materials. Although a strong currency increases the prices of domestically produced goods overseas and in relative terms at home, it may be the case that a stronger currency reduces the price of factor inputs, particularly raw materials and physical capital. If average costs fall, therefore, prices may also be able to become more competitive without sacrificing profit levels.

Similarly, a weak currency can push up import prices and if the price elasticity of demand for imports is low, **imported inflation** can result. It can also be the case that powerful importers decide that cheap output is a threat to their own economic growth and employment levels and particularly where a currency is perceived to be artificially low (e.g. in the case of China and their trade relations with the USA) the importer may make accusations of dumping and impose punitive tariffs to counter the import penetration resulting from lower prices.

A simple encapsulation of the benefits or otherwise of a strong currency can be seen in the survival (and even spectacular success) of some UK manufacturers despite the recent high interest rates, strong currency (these two factors are, of course, linked) and threats from globalisation. The most successful manufacturers include those who have been specialising in adding high levels of value domestically, using highly-skilled labour and capital as appropriate, and the outsourcing or importing of cheap raw materials, components and labour to overseas where possible. Thus strong sterling can benefit a business, providing the right combination of management skill, opportunity and market power exists.

A government must initially decide whether to allow the exchange rate to float, or whether to pursue a fixed or target rate of exchange. If the latter, a suitable and sustainable target must be set and policy instruments applied to achieve it.

Exchange rates determine the prices of internationally traded goods, services, raw materials and components, as well as payments for land and labour. In theory, in a floating regime, the exchange rate will adjust to clear significant surpluses or deficits in the current account, but in reality this can be distorted and delayed by speculation, differences in relative interest rates, and the use of some currencies as a reserve currency in some countries and markets.

Exchange rates influence the balance on the current account, and thus the level of aggregate demand in the economy. This relationship may be complicated, however, by differences between short run and long run adjustments to a weaker or stronger currency: the J-curve and reverse J-curve effects.

Summary questions

1. What are floating exchange rates? What are the advantages of a floating exchange rate regime?

2. What are fixed exchange rates? What are the advantages of a fixed exchange rate regime?

3. Explain the link between interest rates and the equilibrium exchange rate.

4. Explain the short-run and long-run impact of a stronger domestic currency (appreciation) on macroeconomic performance.

5. Explain the short-run and long-run impact of a weaker domestic currency (depreciation) on macroeconomic performance.

Extension questions

A. Why may imported inflation be a particular problem for an economy such as the UK? Which goods and services may contribute the most to higher import prices?

B. Research the concept of Purchasing Power Parity. Does this theory offer an insight into the long-run equilibrium level for an exchange rate? How might speculators use this level to their profit?

C. The 'small country case' is the theoretical position where an economy is unable to determine its own interest rate as any divergence from its 'equilibrium' will immediately create an inflow or outflow of funds which would return the rate to its equilibrium level. What insight does this offer for a concept of equilibrium exchange rates?

Chapter 5

International Trade

The importance of trade

Central to economics is specialisation and trade. Even within the simplest of closed economies, trade can benefit all when households choose to put all their resources into the production of one good or service; this surplus is then traded with other households who have specialised in production in other areas. Adam Smith called this the **division of labour** and modern economies show very high levels of such specialisation. For example, your economics teacher specialises in the production of economics lessons.

International trade, at its simplest level, describes such specialisation between economies or countries. The households and firms within each economy use resources to produce a more limited range of goods and services than are wanted and international markets give the opportunity for mutual benefits from trading these surpluses.

The theory of absolute advantage

Complex ideas in macroeconomics can usually be explained with the use of simple examples. Imagine there are only two economies (Ajax and Barcelona) and the citizens of Ajax and Barcelona produce and consume only two goods (Xylophones and Yeti).

Figure 5.1: Production possibilities

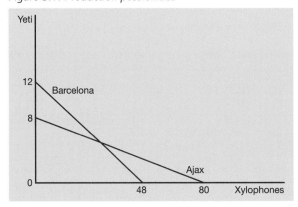

The production possibility frontiers for each of Ajax and Barcelona are shown in Figure 5.1.

Note that the PPFs are straight lines. This implies that the opportunity cost of producing each good in each economy is constant. It appears logical that Ajax is better at producing Xylophones than it is at producing Yeti when compared with Barcelona. To produce one more Yeti in Ajax would require the loss of 10 Xylophones (80/8). On the other hand, in Barcelona the opportunity cost of one more Yeti is only 4 Xylophones (48/12). In absolute terms, Ajax can produce more Xylophones than Barcelona can, and Barcelona can produce more Yeti.

Assuming there is sufficient demand for each of the goods it makes sense for Ajax and Barcelona to specialise on this basis, i.e. for each to produce the good in which they have an absolute advantage.

World production is (in this example) the total production of Ajax and Barcelona combined. Assuming total specialisation takes place, output would be as shown in Table 5.1.

Table 5.1

	Xylophones	**Yeti**
Ajax	80	0
Barcelona	0	12
Total	**80**	**12**

The theory of absolute advantage states that these output levels cannot be improved by any other allocation of resources within the economies. For example, if Ajax and Barcelona each chose to use half of their resources in each industry the total output is shown in Table 5.2.

Table 5.2

	Xylophones	Yeti
Ajax	40	4
Barcelona	24	6
Total	**64**	**10**

The world or total output of both Xylophones and Yeti falls when the economies fail to fully specialise. Both countries therefore benefit from specialisation, assuming effective and stable markets exist to ensure the surpluses produced by each economy can be made available to the other. It was Adam Smith, in his seminal work *The Wealth of Nations*, who first formalised this important economic concept.

But in the example of Ajax and Barcelona, at what price would Xylophones and Yeti be traded? We must look first at the opportunity cost of each good in each economy.

In Ajax, 1 Xylophone costs 1/10 of Yeti. We can write this as

$1\,X = 0.1\,Y$

And in return,

$1\,Y = 10\,X$

In Barcelona, the cost of each good in terms of the other can be expressed as

$1\,X = 0.25\,Y$
$1\,Y = 4\,X$

Thus Ajax will sell Xylophones to Ajax for a price between 0.1 Yeti (the price of Yeti in Ajax if consumed domestically) and 0.25 Y (the price of one Yeti in Barcelona if they produced it themselves). Similarly, Barcelona will sell Yeti for a price between 4 and 10 Xylophones.

The theory of comparative advantage

David Ricardo is credited with the theory of comparative advantage. An admirer of Adam Smith, Ricardo expanded the theory of absolute advantage to show that mutually beneficial trade can take place even when one country has no absolute advantage.

Figure 5.2: More on production possibilities

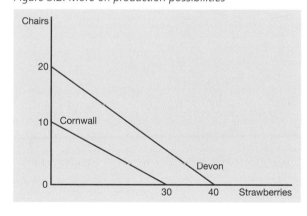

Consider the economies of Cornwall and Devon where again, only two goods are produced: strawberries and chairs. The production possibility frontiers in this case are shown in Figure 5.2.

It would appear that Devon is better at producing both goods than Cornwall. The theory of absolute advantage would suggest that Devon could not benefit from trade with Cornwall. Ricardo's comparative advantage proposes otherwise, and his case can be seen by examining opportunity costs in both economies. Using S for strawberries and C for chairs, the prices of the goods in each country are as follows:

In Cornwall, $1\,S = \frac{1}{3}\,C$ and therefore $1\,C = 3\,S$

In Devon, $1\,S = \frac{1}{2}\,C$ and therefore $1\,C = 2\,S$

Thus Cornwall produces strawberries more cheaply ($\frac{1}{3}$ rather than $\frac{1}{2}$ C) whereas Devon produces chairs more cheaply (2 rather than 3 S). Both economies can gain, therefore, by specialising according to the comparative advantage they enjoy.

The theory of comparative advantage shows why so much trade takes place in the world.

The theory of comparative advantage therefore shows why so much trade takes place in the world. Even small economies with no absolute advantage can find an industry in which they enjoy some degree of comparative advantage. The only exception to the theory is shown in Figure 5.3.

Figure 5.3: No comparative advantage

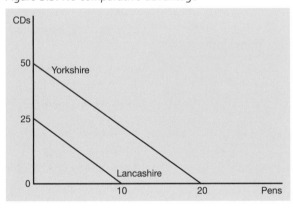

Yorkshire has an absolute advantage in producing both CDs and pens. When examining the opportunity costs of production in each economy, it can be seen that in both Lancashire and Yorkshire the prices are as follows:

1 Pen = 2.5 CDs   and   1 CD = 0.4 Pens

Thus neither economy can produce either good more cheaply than the other.

Weaknesses of absolute and comparative advantage theory

We can identify a number of drawbacks of using these theories to explain patterns of international trade.

PPFs in the real world are not straight

This is another way of saying that opportunity costs are unlikely to be constant. PPFs are usually drawn as concave to the origin (Figure 5.4) to reflect imperfect factor mobility: it is unlikely that all units of land, labour, capital and enterprise are equally productive in all industries. There is also an argument that PPFs may be convex to the origin as in Figure 5.5. As resources become more specialised in their use, their productivity may actually rise. This may be related to the improvement in farmland for particular crops, the

Figure 5.4: Concave production possibilities

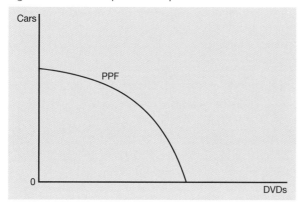

skills and experience of workers and managers, or the investment in specialist machinery. Over time, therefore, the patterns of advantage may shift – or be deliberately shifted – through investment and perseverance (consider, for example, how Japanese manufacturers – and more recently, Chinese producers – have broken into international markets).

Transport costs

Even trade between different regions of one country – and even between, or within, towns and cities – incurs transport costs. This may potentially outweigh any slight comparative or absolute advantage which may exist.

Figure 5.5: Convex production possibilities

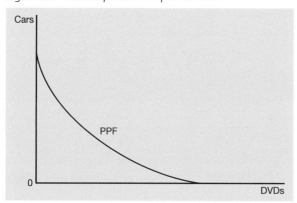

The theories use very simple models

This is certainly true: in reality there are very few cases of two economies producing two goods. This is more of a weakness of two-dimensional paper representation, however – it is possible to build more complex multi-variable examples using computer models.

Goods are rarely homogeneous in the real world

The output of different economies may be of different quality. In the examples above we have assumed that Cornwall's chairs compare equally to those of Devon – and that Devon produces strawberries which compare with those of Cornwall. It may be the case that the climate of each region dictates that the taste, texture, colour, and nutritional content of Cornwall's strawberries are vastly superior – and therefore worthy of a higher price. Perhaps the xylophones of Barcelona are more suited to professional use, rather than the cheap but amateurish output of Ajax. Such information may reduce the simple logic of total specialisation and lead to a much more complex pattern of trade. (A real life example is that of the UK, where exports of electrical motors, generators and transmitters created export volumes of $567m in Q2 of 2007; and imports of the same category of goods were valued at £432m in the same period! Even *within* this apparently narrow category, therefore, some degree of specialisation is possible.)

The model assumes perfect competition

Supernormal profits may close absolute and comparative advantages and make gains from trade less likely. In reality, the global trade of goods and services is often heavily distorted by a lack of competition and protectionist agreements and practices (see the final point below).

Firms and households specialise, not countries

Governments do trade internationally: they buy factors of production from overseas and may sell output to foreigners (consider the output of the BBC, for example, which is sold across the globe), but international trade is far more prevalent in the private sector. A firm is more than its national location – and, in fact, many firms change their 'nationality' to enjoy more favourable tax environments, for example, or to take advantage of necessary labour or raw materials. In addition, labour is not (always) tied to a particular economy. One of the major features of globalisation is international labour movement. This can be seen within the EU where any EU citizen is entitled to freedom of movement to live and work in any other member state.

The role of government, trading blocs and trade agreements

The various forms of protectionism which may distort trade patterns are discussed in the next chapter.

Alternative theories of trade

Aside from an absence of free trade and the weaknesses of the models discussed above, there are other views on the factors which may determine who produces a surplus in what – and who buys it from them.

Factor endowment (Heckscher-Ohlin model)

This model relates to Ricardo's concept of comparative advantage and stresses the importance of *factor endowments*: the natural abundance (or scarcity) of particular quantities and qualities of land, labour, capital and enterprise.

For example, Switzerland has a relatively small land area, some of which comprises snow-covered mountains in the winter. It also has a highly-educated workforce, and its major industries are banking and tourism (e.g. skiing holidays). The Heckscher-Ohlin model would link the suitability of its factors of production to the industries it has nurtured over time.

Economies specialising in agricultural products, then, may not have high education levels but will have a climate particularly suited to the crops grown. Examples might include banana cultivation in India and Brazil, coffee cultivation in Latin America and eastern Africa, and wine from certain regions of France, Italy or Australia.

This model draws heavily on common sense to explain which regions produce particular goods. Obviously oil, diamonds and natural gas can only be extracted in countries which enjoy (economically viable) natural endowments of the commodity. Over time, factor endowments may evolve through natural changes (e.g. an expanding population produces a higher supply of labour) or government policies (investment in infrastructure and new technologies leading to industrialisation).

Switzerland partly specialises in tourism because of its factor endowments.

Competitive advantage

The concept of comparative advantage stresses the importance of relative opportunity costs of production. Competitive advantage focuses more on the actual cost of production and, in reality, firms are concerned with costs, revenues and profits. This approach to the rationale of trade proposes that a firm (and therefore an industry, and an economy) will produce (and trade) where they can do so at a cost which is low enough to compete with similar industries in other countries.

Globalisation has highlighted the growing importance of the multi-national company (MNC) and arguably reduced the importance of the nation state. In the world economy today MNCs are a dominant force in determining what gets produced, how, and who it is sold to. Competitive advantage theory perhaps reflects this trend.

Diversification of risk

The argument in favour of specialisation is that an economy can focus its resources (and, over time, the development of its resources) in the industries to which they are best suited. However, an economy can also over-specialise, particularly in agriculture or tourism where a natural disaster or a shift in tastes can destroy either supply or demand, creating high levels of structural unemployment and poverty. There are also certain industries which all economies may have, regardless of comparative or competitive advantage (see the next chapter on strategic and essential industries).

Similarity preference theory

As discussed above, governments may prefer not to over-specialise, and thus not take full advantage of the best use of its resources. Similarly, consumers may prefer choice when making purchasing decisions. This explains why supermarket shelves are stocked with produce from many different countries, often in direct competition with each other. Some consumers will wish to buy the cheapest coffee or oranges or DVD player, but others are willing to pay a premium for a good which is of higher quality or offers different characteristics. Similarity preference theory explains, therefore, why so many different brands are available from many different countries. In some industries, it is the diversity of country of origin which appeals to consumers (e.g. world cinema, tourism, or financial markets).

Are resources homogeneous?

Finally, it should be mentioned that as well as there being a lack of homogeneity of resources across economies, resources within an economy differ in their suitability. Thus pockets of production in a wide range of industries are likely in all economies where there are suitably qualified and skilled workers with the right technology to produce goods and services for either domestic or overseas consumption.

The case for free trade

The theoretical advantages resulting from *international specialisation and exchange* (mutual gains from trade) provide a theoretical basis for the free trade movement. Closely associated with the growth of globalisation, the case for free trade proposes that a genuine world economy – where all countries focus production in the industries where they are most productive – can benefit all nations and all peoples. The two sides to the argument provide the context to the following two chapters on *protectionism* and *globalisation*.

Summary questions

1. Distinguish carefully between the 'cost' concerned with determining absolute and comparative advantage.

2. Why is specialisation important for successful trade?

3. To what extent do alternative theories of trade, (a) support, and (b) contradict, the importance of absolute and comparative advantage in determining patterns of international trade?

4. What are the main assumptions underlying the theories of absolute and comparative advantage?

5. Is free trade (a) beneficial, and, (b) likely? [It may be useful to return to this question after reading the next two chapters.]

Extension questions

A. Which of the assumptions used in the absolute and comparative advantage are most (un)realistic?

B. What would be the implication of curved production possibility frontiers for comparative advantage?

C. What factors may contribute to changes in comparative advantage over time? Consider possible trends for the UK's comparative advantage and pattern of trade over the next three years.

Chapter 6

Protectionism

Free trade rarely occurs. There have been several attempts and movements in the twentieth century to promote and extend freer international trade, and this chapter will examine the reasons *why* governments or groups of governments (trading blocs) may choose to pursue protectionist policies, and *how* such mechanisms work.

Reasons for protectionism

Macroeconomic stability

Governments may prioritise employment and economic growth in their own economy over the benefits of free trade. In the short-run, trade may be seen as a zero-sum game (purchasing a bottle of wine from South Africa puts a French vineyard owner out of work), and since French voters – and not South Africans – vote in general elections in France, there may be political motives behind protecting domestic industry and therefore jobs.

Essential and strategic industries

The provision of law and order, infrastructure, energy, healthcare and education are key requirements for a modern and stable economy. Even where factors may be more productive in other industries, it may be desirable for an economy to put some resources into these essential industries. In addition, goods such as defence and financial services may be produced domestically in case of international conflict. Within these industries, certain functions may be opened to international trade either fully (e.g. producing military equipment – a speciality of the UK) or partially (e.g. the operations of some banks across the world – perhaps a case of similarity preference?). A classic case of protectionism in agricultural production is the Common Agricultural Policy (CAP) of the European Union.

Infant industry argument

New businesses typically struggle in their early years, but once established may reap economies of scale and these lower average costs allow prices to fall to more competitive levels. Thus the government may subsidise new firms to allow them to grow sufficiently to compete in international markets. However the argument is not a certain one. The infant may not grow up healthily.

Quality of goods argument

The case against cheap imports may be related to the quality of the goods when compared to domestically-produced substitutes. This is an argument often used by more developed countries when restricting imports from cheaper suppliers, for example in the toy industry. Indeed, as shown below, the quality of goods can be used as a means of protectionism.

Ethical issues

Again, often used by consumers or governments in more developed countries, this argument hinges on an assumption that cost advantages enjoyed by manufacturers in some economies may be based on the exploitation of labour. Thus 'sweatshop culture' creates cheap goods at the expense of the human rights of the workers involved.

Dumping is the act of exporting a good at a price below the price in the market.

Anti-dumping policy

Dumping can be defined as the act of exporting a good at a price below the price in the home market (predatory-pricing) or below the cost of production (loss-leading). The first is a case of comparative (or competitive) advantage and is a normal occurrence in (free) markets. The second, however, is more harmful and can justify a reactionary policy. Dumping requires a subsidy, either by a government or a firm willing to trade at a loss in the hope of penetrating a market to create economies of scale over time, or to reduce competition by destroying the domestic producers. The World Trade Organisation (WTO) allows governments to impose a tariff equivalent to the difference between the price charged and the perceived cost of production. This tariff is therefore equal to the subsidy per unit and removes the impact of dumping from the domestic market.

Types of protectionist policies

Figure 6.1: An import tax

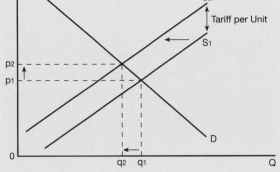

We can identify four types of protectionism: tariffs, quotas, non-tariff barriers and subsidies to home-based producers. We review these in turn.

Tariffs

A tariff is a tax on an import. The impact of a tax is to increase price and reduce the quantity bought and sold (see Figure 6.1).

The tariff raises the price of imported items from p_1 to p_2 and reduces the quantity imported from q_1 to q_2. This should boost

Figure 6.2: The impact of a tariff

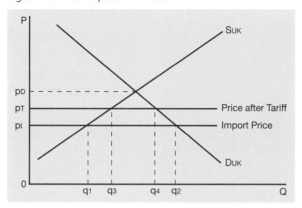

demand for domestic substitutes and thus jobs and growth in the economy are protected at the expense of jobs and growth in the economies of trading partners. We now need to see the impact of a tariff on both the domestic and import markets. This is shown in Figure 6.2.

With no trade, domestic demand would be met only by domestic supply and equilibrium price would be PD. If opened to free trade, import penetration would take place as the world price or import price (PI) is lower than PD. Only domestic suppliers willing and able to produce goods at a price of PI or lower will remain in the market; thus domestic production falls to q1 and (q2-q1) goods will be imported.

A tariff of (PT – PI) per unit increases the price of imports to PT; this allows less efficient domestic suppliers to remain in the market and domestic production increases from q1 to q3. The higher price reduces demand to q3, and thus imports fall from (q1q2) to (q3q4).

Quotas

Quotas work in a similar way to tariffs, increasing the price of imported goods by limiting the quantity of goods allowed into the country. Scarcity increases price and thus a quota (assuming it is set at a level lower than current imports) pushes up import prices and thus, as in Figure 6.2 above, allows more domestic producers to remain in the market at the expense of suppliers from other countries. The welfare implications of higher prices resulting from protection are discussed in the next section below.

One issue of setting quotas is how the limit will affect incentives in the market. For example, if a quota is set at an annual limit there may be a flood of imports early in the year which uses up the quota, creating shortages later. This happened with EU quotas set on Chinese clothing imports in 2005 when the limits were used up mid way through the year, resulting in a block on further imports at European ports. The resulting 'Bra Wars' scenario was only resolved when the EU lifted restrictions and allowed 80 million items of clothing into the EU to avert a clothing shortage.

Regulation and non-tariff barriers

Tariffs and quotas limit quantity by raising price, either directly or indirectly. Other methods of restricting import penetration include imposing high levels of bureaucracy or safety standards on importers. These methods aim to deter imports and/or increase the prices of the goods in the domestic economy by raising costs to suppliers.

Subsidies to domestic producers

One method of lowering domestic costs and prices is for the government to pay subsidies to domestic producers, thus increasing the international competitiveness of their output both at home and in international markets. EU-wide schemes such as the Common Agricultural Policy (CAP) have been criticised for blocking imports in such a way.

The methods explained above aim to protect jobs in the domestic economy through raising the price of imports. However, these higher prices have to be paid by domestic consumers, who may also have less choice in the range of goods and services they can buy. Protectionist measures can therefore be seen to transfer welfare from consumers to producers. This is the case in the EU where consumers face high food prices to protect output, employment and wages in the agricultural industry.

Figure 6.3: Reduced consumer surplus

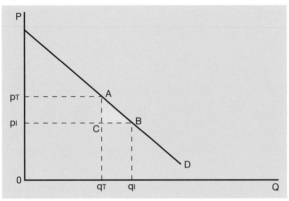

The impact on welfare resulting from protectionism in the case of one commodity can be shown in Figure 6.3, where the shaded area ABC shows the loss of consumer surplus arising from import protection pushing up the price to consumers.

Customs unions: trade creation and trade diversion

A customs union (such as the European Union) is an agreement to abolish internal tariffs whilst maintaining common external tariffs. The impact of joining a customs union will therefore depend on three prices: domestic prices, world prices and the price within the union.

Earlier in the chapter, Figure 6.2 shows how imposing a tariff can protect domestic output and jobs at the expense of higher domestic prices. If the country joined a customs union where such tariffs were abolished, this would reduce prices. This is known as **trade creation**: where membership of a customs union or free trade agreement reduces prices.

It is possible, however, that membership of a customs union increases the price of some goods. This is called **trade diversion** and will occur where the country trades with both members and non-members of the customs union. Prices of non-member imports may actually rise as the common external tariff is applied. Trade diversion may be eradicated if expansion of the customs union can increase specialisation and efficiency to such an extent that members' prices fall to non-member levels. However, where member-produced substitutes are uneconomic or unfeasible (perhaps due to specific factor requirements related to climate or natural resources) trade diversion may persist in the long-run.

Alternatives to protectionism

We need to distinguish between expenditure-switching policies and expenditure-reducing policies.

Expenditure-switching policies

One way of increasing the competitiveness of domestically-produced goods both at home and abroad is devaluation of the currency. In a fixed (or managed) regime this would require a reduction in interest rates or active intervention in the FOREX market (e.g. selling domestic currency and buying more of the currency the authorities wish to devalue against). Under floating exchange rates such intervention may also take place but it will be undertaken informally and is sometimes known as 'dirty floating'. A weaker currency increases the prices of imported goods and decreases the price of exports. The short-run and long-run impacts of this were discussed in greater detail in Chapter 4 (see the J-curve and Marshall-Lerner condition).

The main problem with a competitive devaluation is that it is only effective where the other country or countries are fully committed to a fixed regime; otherwise the other economy can reduce interest rates or sell their own currency until the exchange rate returns to its original level.

Expenditure-reducing policies

An alternative to expenditure-switching is expenditure-reducing. Current account deficits can arise from high economic growth: the economy sucks in imports when domestic production is unable to meet the level of domestic demand. In addition, as incomes rise the demand for luxury goods will rise disproportionately (the income elasticity of demand for luxuries is greater than for necessities) and these may be produced abroad. An example would be luxury holidays which tend to be imported from economies with sunnier climates and exotic scenery.

The main disadvantage of expenditure-reducing is the deflationary impact on the economy. Reducing imports with this method involves slowing economic growth, which may benefit the current account (and inflation, if this is a problem) but it will increase unemployment and will probably put pressure on government finances through fiscal drag. Therefore expenditure-reducing will only be used *in extremis*. In addition, reducing economic activity may also harm domestic production, and thus imports. If slowdown is achieved through higher taxes or higher interest rates this can reduce investment in both cases, thus harming the long-run productive potential of the economy.

Increasing international competitiveness

Aside from lowering the exchange rate, the competitiveness of domestically-produced goods (both at home and abroad) can be increased in various other ways:

▶ Keeping domestic inflation below price increases in competitor economies

▶ Encouraging competition and efficiency in domestic goods and labour markets

▶ Improving infrastructure to assist the ability of manufacturers to keep down costs

▶ Raising productivity through higher educational standards and enhanced skills

▶ Cutting bureaucracy and regulation to help producers contain costs

Summary questions

1. What are the main reasons for protectionism?

2. Why may protectionist policies increase rather than decrease during a period of increasing globalisation?

3. Using diagrams for each, explain how the following can reduce the levels of imports into a country: (a) tariffs, (b) quotas, (c) regulation, (d) subsidies to domestic producers.

4. Explain the likely impact of protectionism on social welfare.

5. Explain one disadvantage of each of the following policies: (a) expenditure-reducing, (b) expenditure-switching.

Extension questions

A. Research a current or recent trade dispute where protectionism (threatened or actual) has been an issue. What are the apparent reasons/justifications for protectionism in this case?

B. What is meant by dumping? Why is dumping difficult to prove and can it ever be justified?

C. 'Safety standards in developed countries are a harmful form of protectionism.' To what extent do you agree with this statement?

Chapter 7

The Economics of Globalisation

Introduction to globalisation

Globalisation is a broad term which describes changes in the volume of trade, growth and migration in the world economy. Although there have been rapid increases in these factors throughout history, globalisation in a modern sense refers to developments seen since the 1990s.

Globalisation is used to describe a very wide variety of changes, some of which are cultural (the 'Americanisation' of music, film and retail, for example). Those concerned primarily with economics include a large number of phenomena relating to international exchange. Here are several inter-related aspects:

▶ Increased influence of powerful corporations (MNCs: Multinational Corporations) operating in a large number of countries

▶ Falling barriers to trade resulting in increased levels of trade between countries and geographical areas (this includes trade in raw materials, components, energy, semi-finished goods, as well as finished goods and services)

▶ Increasing homogeneity of safety standards in goods markets

▶ Increased international capital investment flows

▶ Increased levels of labour migration and the resulting emergence of a global workforce (at both ends of the skills spectrum)

▶ Rapid spread of new technologies, manufacturing systems and management techniques

▶ Faster communication and information flows and the resulting emergence of 'new' markets

▶ Opening of trade with areas traditionally limited in their exporting and importing of goods (e.g. China, the former Soviet Union countries)

▶ Newly-Industrialising Countries (NICs) taking the place of traditional economic superpowers in the secondary sector of the world economy

▶ Falling costs of air and sea transport and travel and freight costs, associated with greater competition and choice in related markets

The cause and effect in the above factors is complex. Supporters and critics of globalisation would highlight the interrelated and unregulated nature of many of these developments as being either a positive or negative point respectively!

Arguments in favour of globalisation

Increased global wealth
The law of comparative advantage states that gains from trade can occur in almost any situation; thus there has been a free trade movement (led by agencies such as the World Trade Organisation) to promote and extend the benefits of unrestricted trade to as many countries as possible.

Faster economic development
The 'Washington Consensus' (the free market views of the World Trade Organisation and the International Monetary Fund) on the advantages of free trade links faster economic growth with faster economic development. Globalisation may be linked to increases in democracy (including political, gender and personal freedoms) and knowledge about democratic possibilities, reductions in child labour, falling infant mortality and increases in life expectancy. Such are the tangible benefits of economic progress.

Large corporations can reduce average costs by spreading overheads over higher levels of output.

Economies of scale

Larger corporations can spread overheads over higher levels of output, reducing average costs and allowing prices to fall. In addition, businesses can move their global headquarters to countries with lower rates of corporation tax.

Greater competition and choice

Better information on prices and costs allows households, firms and governments to make more informed consumption and production decisions. This leads to productive and allocative efficiency (assuming perfect competition) and a wider range of higher quality goods available to all.

Arguments against globalisation

Greater inequality

The gains from trade may not always be distributed evenly throughout an economy. Economics studies the creation and distribution of rising incomes and wealth, and even if critics of globalisation concede that the phenomenon can lead to wealth creation, it is the division of the spoils which remains cause for concern. If profits rise faster than wages, it is argued that labour is being exploited and underpaid and inequality in developing countries may increase. There have also been recent high-profile scandals such as those regarding the use of child labour to manufacture branded clothing for Western nations.

Environmental impacts

Opponents of globalisation have criticised Western firms for shifting production to developing or newly industrialising countries where environmental regulation may be less strict; thus exporting environmental problems overseas. This 'environmental dumping' contributes to global problems such as climate change whilst allowing the home countries to achieve domestic emissions targets. In addition, local environmental problems may arise from the degradation of natural habitats. In some cases this may provide a trade-off between short-run gains in employment and economic growth versus the declining potential to enjoy and profit from such habitats, for example through tourism.

Reduced competition and choice (homogeneity)

The argument that globalisation increases choice by forcing brands to compete in wider international markets assumes that the total number of firms increases. However, it may be the case that competition actually declines as powerful firms buy up their competitors to create global monopolies and oligopolies. It may then be possible for these firms to increase prices to reduce the welfare of consumers in both the developed and developing world.

Greater vulnerability to exogenous shocks

As markets become increasingly interlinked and interdependent, it may be assumed that a downturn in one area of the world economy will have an increasing impact on all other regions. There are two contradictory arguments here. On the one hand, globalisation allows all countries to absorb exogenous shocks more easily. For example, if a firm is supplying only a small number of countries it follows that a downturn or recession in one of these nations will have a large impact on their demand and profit levels. Thus firms supplying a larger number of countries will be less vulnerable to a downturn in any one of them. On the other hand, the convergent nature of many economies, particularly within a geographical region such as mainland Europe means all economies are affected by any exogenous shock. Hence, it is likely that a slowdown in one country is likely to be linked to – or spread quickly to – all other economies.

The impact of globalisation on the UK economy

The UK enjoyed strong economic growth over the decade between 1997 and 2007. During this period unemployment was either falling or at very low levels, alongside low and stable inflation.

Figure 7.1: UK business investment (£bn)

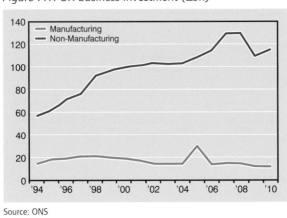

Source: ONS

Figure 7.2: UK household consumption and total GDP, 2006 prices (£bn)

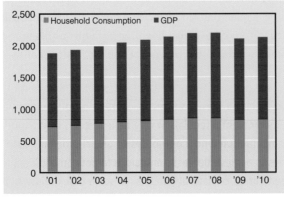

Source: ONS

One contributing factor to low inflation in the UK was the benefits brought via globalisation: cheap raw materials and finished goods imported from low wage-cost countries. In addition, the influx of foreign workers to industries as diverse as agriculture, factory work, construction and hospitality and catering reduced domestic firms' costs, allowing UK prices to remain under control despite strong demand and a tight domestic labour market. Globalisation therefore appeared to allow supply-side growth in the economy (rising world productivity shifting out the LRAS and PPF curve).

Low inflation also allowed interest rates to remain at historically low levels, creating a boom in aggregate demand through encouraging consumption and investment.

The downside of cheap credit was rising levels of debt (household, business and government) and the impact of a consumer boom on the current account. As demand outstripped supply the economy sucked in more and more imports and the current account moved into a very large deficit. Figure 7.3 shows the rapid expansion in consumer credit in recent years.

Figure 7.3: Annual growth in consumer credit in UK (year on year, %)

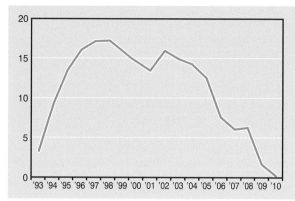

Source: ONS

Figure 7.4: Current account balance, 2006 prices (£bn)

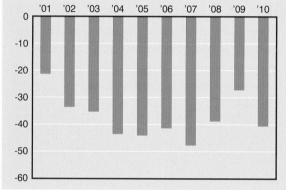

Source: ONS

Figure 7.4 shows two contrasting trends on the current account over the last 15 years. Between 1992 (when sterling left the ERM) and 1997, economic growth was accompanied by an improvement in the current account – suggesting an export-led recovery resulting from a weaker currency. From 1998, however, the current account worsened for three years as imports increased dramatically relative to exports; this trend as countered in the early 2000s by economic uncertainty relating to the end of the dot com boom and other events, but since then the UK continued to experience a widening gap between exports and imports until the recent recession.

Globalisation lowers costs for businesses and this helps to control inflation, but at the possible expense of job losses for domestic workers, either through the influx of cheap (and possibly better skilled and trained workers) labour from overseas or the outsourcing of some or all of UK output to countries where all factors of production are cheaper. Recent data suggests that over half of the new jobs created in the UK in 2010 went to foreign-born workers.

Until the recession, it was often argued that developed economies suffered the least, and arguably gained the most, from globalisation. Even after the catastrophic events of the Credit Crunch, UK and US firms dominate the global banking system, but growth in this area over the last decade has perhaps come at the expense of decline in other sectors. Manufacturing firms have found the challenge of meeting global competition more difficult to meet in markets where a greater degree of competition exists and foreign goods are comparable in quality. Manufacturing in Western economies looks to be increasingly specialist and, perhaps, foreign-owned.

The tendency for manufacturing industry to be geographically concentrated can exacerbate the problem of globalisation for some areas of the UK. Structural unemployment exists where workers' skills are no longer relevant to the jobs currently vacant, and this most typically occurs when an industry declines, as would be the case if foreign competition becomes intense enough to drive out domestic producers from the market. Thus regional inequality can also be a side-effect of globalisation, with attendant problems of factor immobility as households become locked into low-wage, low house price areas as they cannot afford to move to the (more expensive) areas where jobs are available and more highly-paid. This is particularly true in a housing market such as the UK where owner-occupying is far more prevalent than renting. It may also lead to a 'brain drain' of the more highly-skilled and educated workers to industries and areas of the country which are enjoying stronger growth.

The impact of globalisation on developing countries

Globalisation is often seen as a process of the loss of Western jobs and output to rapidly developing economies such as China and India. However, there are also fears in developing and newly-industrialising countries that globalisation brings its own problems and issues.

As with economies such as the UK, there will be winners and losers in developing countries. It is likely that inequality will widen as some households and entrepreneurs are able to take advantage of opportunities more than others. Again, there may be geographical concentrations of winners and losers. In China, for example, much of the economic growth experienced in recent years has been concentrated in the Zhujiang and Yangtze river deltas and the Bohai Sea rim, creating a divergence of income levels when compared with other regions.

Similarly, some countries will gain more than others. Those with a reputation for strong government and a transparent commercial sector – and with a clear comparative advantage and the ability to exploit this – are far more likely to profit in a world economy experiencing greater openness to trade and competition.

Newly-industrialising countries (NICs) in particular are emerging as effective competitors in manufacturing sectors traditionally associated with Western producers. The BRIC group of nations (Brazil, Russia, India, China) are usually cited as the most likely success stories of globalisation beyond the West; their comparative advantages appear to be in raw materials (such as timber), energy, services and manufactured goods respectively – although the true patterns of trade are, as usual, far more complex than this stereotype suggests.

One limitation to the benefits of globalisation in the developing world is the repatriation of profits. Multinational companies have moved some or all of their functions across the globe but the majority of their shareholders (and therefore ultimate beneficiaries of their profits) are located in the West; in addition, their most senior managers are usually expatriate workers who will repatriate their incomes at some stage, and hence the benefits to the domestic economy may be more limited than first appears.

China has a comparative advantage in manufactured goods and makes most of the world's clocks.

Nonetheless, MNCs do create jobs wherever they locate, and they may also partly or fully fund improvements in local infrastructure and education. Thus there may be positive externalities linked to their presence, which may be countered by problems such as pollution and congestion associated with extractive and manufacturing industries or inequality resulting from wage differentials between traditional work and those offered by MNCs.

A worst-case scenario may be a temporary comparative advantage as a cheap-land, cheap-labour 'landlord economy' which attracts MNC interest for as long as the low costs persist; once local living standards rise to a point at which a cheaper location is available, the MNC leaves and structural unemployment may arise. It is the more dynamic governments and entrepreneurs who will be able to prevent this. China, for example, is encouraging entrepreneurial activity to help create Chinese brands in, for example, clothing, rather than just hope an MNC will stay there indefinitely.

Other problems may be associated with the wages paid by MNCs in developing countries. As much of the attraction of the locations lies in cheap factors of production, it is by definition that MNCs will seek to pay wages lower than those paid in the West. This may be exacerbated if an MNC dominates a local labour market and is able to use their monopsony power to keep wages low, with or without the complicity of local governments.

A final issue for both developing and developed economies is that of trade conflict. As the hegemony of Western dominance in world trade is threatened, some countries and trading blocs are turning to more and more protectionist policies to limit import penetration and maintain domestic employment levels. This can be especially true in periods of recession, where protectionism can be tempting as a short-run fix to lost output and jobs, regardless of the long-run implications.

International organisations associated with globalisation and free trade

The promotion of globalisation and free trade is associated with several organisations such as the World Bank, the International Monetary Fund and the World Trade Organisation. The **World Bank** was established in 1945 to provide funds for national development and reduce poverty. As of 2011 it has 187 members and it works primarily with developing countries to aid the creation of a business environment and infrastructure necessary in a successful economy. The **International Monetary Fund** (IMF) oversees the world financial system and aims to stabilise exchange rates and promote stable payment systems between economies. The **World Trade Organisation** (WTO) was established in 1995 to reduce poverty through the promotion of free trade.

The World Bank and IMF are sometimes criticised for their so-called 'Washington consensus' on the policies promoted for reform in the developing world. These include careful fiscal discipline, privatisation and deregulation, trade liberalisation and possibly competitive currency devaluation. The free market doctrine which underpins this is often criticised as conducive to exploitation by developed countries and their MNCs, perhaps at the expense of genuine growth and poverty reduction in the developing countries themselves. The IMF has been a focus of the anti-globalisation movement, criticised heavily for failing to respond quickly and effectively enough to crises and hindering developing countries with high levels of debt and punitive conditions attached to such borrowing.

Similarly, the World Trade Organisation is sometimes perceived as a cheerleader for Western capitalism, and as such benefits consumers and firms in developed countries more than those in NICs or the developing world. Criticism focuses on the allocation of voting rights in the decision-making process (apparently benefitting large, developed economies) and the slow breakdown of protectionism in the developed world, in particular asymmetric trends in agricultural protection where developing countries appear to be under pressure to open their markets faster than developed countries seem willing to. In addition, anti-dumping tariffs supported by the WTO have been used mainly by developed countries, although this trend may change as more developing countries choose to penalise their trading partners in this way.

Table 7.1: The most globalised economies in the world (2009)

1	Singapore
2	Hong Kong (SAR)
3	Ireland
4	Belgium
5	Sweden
6	Denmark
7	Switzerland
8	The Netherlands
9	Israel
10	Finland

Source: Ernst & Young (2010)

Key concerns of the anti-globalisation movement are workers' rights in the developing world, macroeconomic implications for developed nations, and the environment. Globalisation has seen manufacturing processes spread across the world and this industrialisation and urbanisation has had far-reaching consequences for people, habitats and communities. Defenders of traditional societies and environments exist in both developed and developing countries, and the success of the arguments posited will influence patterns of growth, trade and development in the decades ahead.

Summary questions

1. Choose three trends used to identify (economic) globalisation. To what extent are these trends linked?

2. Which groups (in both developed and developing countries) may most benefit from changes associated with globalisation?

3. Which groups (in both developed and developing countries) may be most vulnerable to changes associated with globalisation?

4. With reference to typical macroeconomic objectives (real output and growth, inflation, unemployment, budget position, the current account) outline possible benefits and threats to the UK of globalisation.

5. How might Tanzania and India (both developing countries) perceive different threats and benefits from globalisation?

Extension questions

A. Evaluate the performance of the WTO and the World Bank in supporting economic growth and economic development in the developing world.

B. With reference to Table 7.1, identify similarities and differences between the countries which are regarded as being most economically globalised.

C. A paper produced by Goldman Sachs in 2003 proposed an N-11 ('Next Eleven') group of economies to have the potential to be the next BRICS. Research this group and consider which are most likely to experience significant growth and development.

Chapter 8

The UK and the European Economy

Single European market and customs union

The European Union is a **customs union** where there is freedom of trade (no tariffs and quotas) in goods and services, freedom of movement of labour and capital between member countries, and common external tariffs on imports from outside the union. Thus France and Spain impose no protectionism on each other's goods, but both impose (for example) an 8.8% tariff on kiwifruit from New Zealand.

Trade requires specialisation, and freedom of trade should allow countries to specialise in those industries in which they enjoy a comparative advantage. There are both static and dynamic gains from free trade: static gains arise from specialisation at a point in time and dynamic gains occur as the comparative advantage is strengthened over time by increased productivity through education, training and investment in relevant infrastructure and technologies.

EU enlargement

The EU has experienced both deepening and widening in recent years. Deepening has occurred as the economic, political and social links of member countries and their populations and industry have grown stronger. Widening has occurred as membership of the EU has expanded. Ten countries joined in 2004 (Cyprus, Czech Republic, Estonia, Hungary, Latvia, Lithuania, Malta, Romania, Slovakia and Slovenia) and a further two were added in 2007 (Bulgaria and Romania) to take the total number of members to 27.

In theory, enlargement has increased the opportunities for specialisation and trade. In particular, the factor endowments of both agricultural land and skilled labour have added to the resources of the European Union and thus increase its productive potential. The perceived benefit of these countries joining the EU depends on the assumption that a collective use of the resources will create higher total output than if they remain outside the customs union and single market.

However, the freedom of movement of capital and labour can be seen as a threat to more established (and probably higher cost) producers in Western Europe. Migration between member states can affect local labour and housing markets and add pressure to public services. Factors of production, if unobstructed, will move to their highest value uses, but there are significant labour market imperfections and cultural and language factors which may prevent, say, low-skilled workers in the UK moving to Poland or Bulgaria to enjoy the lower cost of living which would be more suitable given their low earning potential. This dimension of freedom of movement of labour is rarely considered and migration is seen as a one-way process. The exception is perhaps the phenomenon of Britons retiring abroad, funded by the sale of expensive property relative to some other parts of the EU in crowded Britain and the purchase of cheaper housing in mainland Europe.

European institutions

The European Commission (EC) is responsible for legislation and decision-making and the day-to-day running of the EU. It is headed by the President who is one of the commissioners. Each member state enjoys a single representative.

The European Central Bank (ECB) operates as any other central bank. It sets monetary policy for the 15 members of the eurozone. As such, its work is often at the heart of arguments regarding, say, UK adoption of the euro to replace sterling. As of January 2011, the subset of EU countries (known as the euro zone or the euro area) who are now using the euro as their primary currency is now 17-strong (Austria, Belgium, Cyprus, Estonia, Finland, France, Germany, Greece, Ireland, Italy, Luxembourg, Malta, Netherlands,

Portugal, Slovakia, Slovenia, Spain). The main arguments in favour of a single European currency are as follows:

Advantages of European Monetary Union

There are several theoretical gains arising from monetary union.

(Even) greater trade

The single currency acts as a fixed exchange rate (encouraging certainty regarding relative costs and prices) and also removes the transaction costs incurred when changing currencies (any import duties [tariffs] have already been removed through membership of the customs union). This should further stimulate intra-eurozone trade. Previously, any comparative advantage had to be sufficient to cover both exchange and transport costs between countries. With a single currency only the transport cost needs to be considered, and thus greater opportunities for gains from trade should arise.

Dynamic gains

As patterns of greater trade arise, regions and countries can reinforce specialisms through related eduction and training, infrastructure and technology.

Lower inflation

The growth in trade, specialisation and competition within the eurozone should help keep prices low and reduce inflationary pressure. This may allow the ECB to keep base rates low and stimulate still higher levels of economic growth.

Devaluation is not an option

Adoptees of a single currency can no longer devalue against each other as a short-run solution to deal with declining international competitiveness. (This can also be seen as a disadvantage!) In theory, however, this inability to devalue may force households, firms and governments to increase productivity and raise the quality of output to compete in the more demanding EU trading environment.

'Bigger is stronger'

A larger and more diverse economic area is less vulnerable to exogenous shocks and speculative currency attack. This view is debatable and fears over a more globalised economy often focus on the rapid spread of both negative and positive economic impacts. In addition, work on the optimal nature of monetary union areas may highlight the limitations for Europe in adopting a single currency.

Disadvantages of European Monetary Union

Despite these possible advantages from monetary union they need to be compared with some inherent problems arising from such membership.

'One size fits all' monetary policy

A currency has a single base rate of interest, usually set or controlled by the central bank. For the eurozone, the ECB sets the base rate and this applies to all countries. This criticism of EMU usually highlights the problem of cutting rates when most countries are experiencing slowdown or recession, whilst members with stronger currencies may experience inflationary pressure – and thus the policy suits some countries and not others. However, adoption of the Euro requires convergence criteria to be met by member countries. These criteria look for evidence that the economic cycle and other economic indicators of members are aligned. Of course, this does not preclude or prevent shocks which may affect one member more than others, or a more gradual drift apart which would put pressure on central policy-making.

Note that the UK currently also has a 'one-size fits all' policy with base rates in the sense it applies to all parts of the UK. There is a strong argument that the relatively high interest rates in recent years (when compared to other countries) have been appropriate for controlling inflation and the housing market in south-eastern England. But in other regions where manufacturing is of greater importance than in the south-east of England the impact of high interest rates has caused concern about the ability of manufacturers to compete with other countries.

Loss of policy instruments

Monetary policy is ceded from the national central bank to the ECB, and devaluation (against other eurozone members) is no longer an option. The Stability and Growth Pact also sets a maximum budget deficit of 3% in any given year. This limits domestic policy instruments and makes the achievement of all macroeconomic objectives (growth, inflation, unemployment, current account) difficult. The Tinbergen principle states that to achieve, say, four objectives, the government requires four policy instruments. Supporters of EMU would argue that the ECB has an inflation target and the loss of control for national government and monetary authorities is balanced by a loss of responsibility. The importance and effectiveness of successful convergence criteria becomes crucial in this argument.

EMU will be inflationary, EMU will be deflationary

The inflationary argument is that movement to a new currency allows retailers to increase prices, taking advantage of imperfect knowledge and often difficult calculations regarding exchange rates between the old and new currency. Interestingly, the Maltese authorities at the time of its membership required all retailers to publish prices in both Euros and Maltese Pounds for a period before adopting the Euro in the hope that this would improve information and prevent the exploitation of consumers.

The deflationary argument is often used in the UK when comparing the ECB target of inflation (CPI < 2% p.a.) with the higher target used by the Monetary Policy Committee of the Bank of England, the implication being that growth will be lower in the eurozone than if the UK retains sterling. Supporters of EMU would argue that inflationary pressures are genuinely higher in the UK, not least due to asset-price inflation linked to a more volatile housing market and a higher tendency to fund consumer spending with debt rather than income.

Contagion and crisis

In late 2009 it began to be apparent that the economy of Greece was facing serious difficulties. The government budget deficit was found to be in excess of 12% of GDP, considerably higher than previous official figures, and Greek national debt was some 120% of GDP.

A series of fiscal austerity measures have been attempted in Greece to control government spending but these have proved politically unpopular, even though bailout funds from the EU have been tied to fiscal reform. Some economists argue that the example of Greece is evidence that a large single currency area is unsustainable and even apparently converged economies will inevitably drift apart over time. Pro-European and pro-eurozone economists argue that the severity of the financial crisis and recession in the late 2000s was a special case and perhaps greater fiscal (as well as monetary) harmonisation is required to ensure all governments act responsibly. There are also plans for an emergency European Monetary Fund to provide assistance to correct imbalances within the eurozone during times of crisis.

The sovereign debt crises experienced to varying degrees in the PIIGS economies (Portugal, Italy, Ireland, Greece and Spain) have brought into question the whole idea of monetary union. It has been argued by some economists that the variance in economic performance within the Eurozone is simply too great and more freedom and independence, rather than more conformity, is required. Critics of the Euro have been quick to suggest that recent events and crises will even lead to a break up of the Eurozone and a return to individual national currencies.

The concept of Optimal Currency Areas offers a useful analysis of the suggested requirements for successful monetary union.

Optimal currency areas

The pioneering work of Robert Mundell and Abba Lerner (the latter of Marshall-Lerner fame) has identified the optimal or necessary conditions for successful monetary union. These include:

▶ Labour mobility (including the absence of linguistic, legal and cultural barriers to movement)

▶ Capital mobility

▶ A redistributive mechanism for transferring funds between the 'winners' and 'losers' from trade and specialisation

▶ Absence or rarity of asymmetric shocks

Whilst the eurozone meets some of these criteria, it does not meet all of them. The single market allows freedom of movement of capital and labour, and EU structural funds redirect spending to less buoyant regions by improving, for example, transport infrastructure (including projects in parts of the UK). Opponents of EMU in the UK usually focus on the lack of common language and the differences between economic cycles in the UK (which may be more closely linked to economic trends in the USA, for example) and mainland Europe.

More recent work on optimal currency areas suggests that the cause and effect between a common currency and these criteria may be highly complex. Indeed, adopting a single currency may be a strong precursor to satisfying the conditions necessary for a currency area to be optimal.

The UK and Europe: comparative statistics

Figure 8.1: Real GDP (annual % growth)

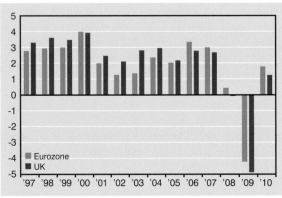

Source: HM Treasury

Figure 8.2: CPI inflation (%, year on year)

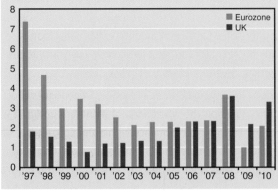

Source: HM Treasury

1992 marked an important year for the UK and EMU. Sterling crashed out of the Exchange Rate Mechanism and if at first economists felt this would be disastrous for British economic prospects, the story that has emerged since provides a fascinating contrast between a major European economy and the core nations of Europe and the eurozone. Macroeconomic performance, as ever, can be judged on the basis of the key variables of growth, prices, jobs, current account and the savings ratio. We consider each of these variables in turn.

Throughout the early years of the NICE decade the UK economy grew more rapidly than the eurozone average. However, from 2006 this trend reversed and the UK suffered a deeper recession. So far, too, the UK recovery has been more fragile. It should be noted, however, that growth rates vary greatly across the eurozone and the PIIGS nations (Portugal, Ireland, Italy, Greece and Spain) have budget deficit and national debt levels which are worryingly high. The Coalition government formed in the UK in 2010 has put in place an austerity plan to cut government spending and close the fiscal gap by 2014-15.

The trend in inflation since 1997 shows a similar story. The Non-Inflationary aspect of the NICE decade is clear to see in Figure 8.2, with CPI well within the limits of 1% either side of 2% per annum between 2001 and 2007. Throughout the recession, however, inflation in the UK has remained stubbornly high as weaker sterling has caused imported inflation and increases in global food and oil prices have pushed up prices generally. It should be noted that CPI (as of mid-2011) is significantly above the top limit of 3%, yet the Monetary Policy Committee of the Bank of England has maintained the historically low base rate level of 0.5%. The MPC is treading a fine line between sustaining recovery and retaining the possibility of a rise in base rate at a point where greater demand poses a serious threat of driving inflation even higher.

Figure 8.3: Unemployment (%)

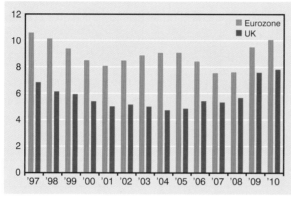

Source: HM Treasury

Figure 8.4: Current account on the balance of payments (% of GDP)

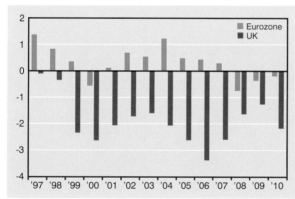

Source: HM Treasury

Figure 8.5: UK consumer credit and retail sales growth (% annual change)

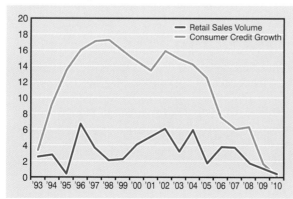

Source: HM Treasury

On unemployment, the UK is clearly a strong performer when compared to the eurozone average shown in Figure 8.3. The UK has generally more flexible labour markets than many of its European partners and this has helped firms to absorb the fall in demand during the recent recession and continue to create new jobs through the recovery. The years ahead will be crucial for the UK labour market. As government spending cuts inevitably lead to losses in public sector employment, the extent to which the skills of these workers will be sufficiently transferable to allow them to take advantage of job creation in the private sector will be crucial in avoiding significant structural unemployment.

The UK's current account remains a concern. The recession reduced the UK's propensity to suck in imports from international markets, but as can be seen in Figure 8.4 the deficit widened once again in 2010. Some of the fall in the deficit can be explained by the fall in the value of sterling (see Figures 4.4 and 4.5 in Chapter 4). Mervyn King, the Governor of the Bank of England, has stated the need for the UK to shift from consumption, borrowing and importing towards greater saving and exporting.

The consumer credit boom which characterised the NICE decade in the mid-2000s is clear to see in Figure 8.5. Cheap money and easy lending fuelled increases in borrowing (and a massive decline in saving) and a housing boom. Note that the retail sales data is more volatile. In 2005 there was a dip in retail sales volume growth linked to a slowdown in real GDP growth, before the economy picked up again for another two years before the credit crisis and recession pushed credit and retail sales growth towards zero.

To return to the issue of saving in the UK, the dramatic decline in the saving ratio (see Figure 8.6) reflects what has been happening behind the scenes of the key macroeconomic policy objectives in recent years.

Over the course of the NICE decade, UK households saved a lower and lower proportion of their income. This happened for a variety of reasons:

▶ Lower interest rates creating a lower incentive to save.

▶ Lower interest rates creating an increase in consumer demand.

▶ Greater access to lending for a wider range of borrowers (most significantly, the 'subprime' mortgage market in the USA).

▶ Diversion of funds from traditional saving mechanisms (such as pensions) towards more speculative activity on the UK housing market.

Figure 8.6: UK household saving ratio (% of income)

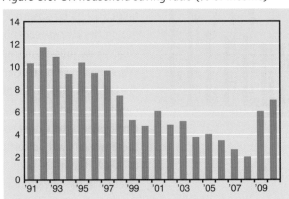

Source: HM Treasury

In comparison with most of continental Europe, the UK has a much higher proportion of owner-occupied housing. This gives the housing market a far more significant impact on household wealth in the UK. It can also lead to lower geographical labour mobility.

The Credit Crunch is discussed in more detail in Chapter 10.

Summary questions

1. How might a single market encourage specialisation and trade?

2. Explain one economic benefit and one economic cost of EU enlargement to both a new and an existing member of the EU.

3. Outline the key economic advantages of a country such as the UK adopting the euro.

4. To what extent does a knowledge of optimal currency area theory support the UK position as a member of the EU but not a member of the eurozone?

5. Why have UK households spent more and saved less than the EU average in recent years?

Extension questions

A. What are the convergence criteria and conditions of entry established by both the European monetary authorities and the present government regarding possible UK adoption of the euro?

B. Under what conditions, if any, should the UK adopt the euro as its currency?

C. What would be the implications for the rest of the Eurozone, and the UK, of a country leaving the single currency?

Chapter 9

Economic Development

Measuring economic development

The terms economic growth and economic development are often used interchangeably but the two terms refer to different concepts. Economic growth refers to changes in GDP which provide a measure, even when adjusted for changes in prices and changes in population, which gives a limited perspective on the actual living standards and life experience of individuals within an economy. Economic development is a broader issue and relates to structural changes in both quantitative factors (average incomes, life expectancy and productivity) and qualitative factors (such as industrial diversity, consumer choice and opportunity). Thus economic growth measures increases in the standard of living; economic development measures the wider concept of quality of life. Economic growth may aid economic development but development requires more than simply higher levels of GDP.

Table 9.1: Comparative data on GDP per capita and HDI (2010)

Rank Order	Human Development Index (United Nations, 2010)	GDP per capita ranking (IMF, 2010)
1	Norway	4
2	Australia	10
3	New Zealand	32
4	United States	7
5	Ireland	13
6	Liechtenstein	2 (CIA Factbook)
7	Netherlands	9
8	Canada	12
9	Sweden	14
10	Germany	19
26	United Kingdom	21
65	Russia	52
73	Brazil	71
89	China	94
169	Zimbabwe	180

Source: UN, IMF

Human Development Index

The Human Development Index is calculated by the UN for 177 countries (some nations are not included, due to lack of willingness and/or ability to provide data) and aims to put human and social issues rather than economic data at the heart of development. HDI is a composite index in that it combines data on three indicators, one economic and the other two non-monetary indicators:

▶ **Income** (measured as GDP per capita adjusted for purchasing power parity)

▶ **Life expectancy** (measured as average years of life, from birth)

▶ **Educational attainment** (measured as a combination of adult literacy and participation in primary, secondary and tertiary education)

Countries can then be ranked and compared with each other, and in addition the HDI sets minimum and maximum levels (goalposts) for each measure against which each country can be compared:

▶ **Income** (US$100-US$40,000)

▶ **Life expectancy** (25-85 years)

▶ **Educational attainment** (0%-100%, both measures)

HDI therefore aims to offer a broader measure of well-being and welfare than only using GDP.

Criticisms of HDI

A complex index will always struggle to represent individual economic and social experiences and criticisms of the HDI measure focus on two main areas: statistical and ranking problems, and omitted (but valid) influences on welfare.

Inequality within countries

Any aggregate (or average) measure of income or development may mask unequal and/or unfair distributions across the population. For example, high adult illiteracy and low life expectancy may be concentrated in certain groups (perhaps related to gender, religion or ethnicity) because of unequal access to education and healthcare.

Unequal clustering of data

In terms of life expectancy, the data for the top 40 countries has a range of approximately 11 years with a minimum of 68.8 years (Hungary) and a maximum of 79.9 years (Iceland); for GDP the top performer (Norway US$41,420) has a figure over three times greater than the lowest (Chile, $12,027); in terms of educational attainment the adult illiteracy rate is very low for most of the top 40 countries but rises as high as, for example, 12.1% in Malta. Critics of HDI have highlighted these proportional disparities and the non-linear relationships between income, education and health.

Similarly, the difference between life opportunities and welfare between, say, 1st and 40th place and 101st and 140th means the data should be interpreted with caution.

Omitted and misrepresented measures of development

Several aspects of the quality of life can be identified which are not included in the HDI. For example:

▶ **Crime** has a dramatic effect on welfare (in countries such as the UK as well as, say, Kenya). Although violent crime will, *in extremis*, reduce life expectancy, low level crime and a lack of social cohesion will be generally unrepresented in HDI data.

▶ **Externalities** such as pollution and congestion may lower life expectancy but the full costs of industrial activity may be more extensive. Many developed countries now outsource heavy (and thus dirty) industry to developing and newly industrialising countries – and thus to some extent outsourcing premature death and ill health in the process.

▶ **Types of public services provided:** a country which spends a significant proportion of tax revenues on education should, arguably, be more highly ranked than one which spends large levels on weapons of mass destruction. Yet, (except for indirectly through impacts on the variables that are measured) this will not be treated any differently by the HDI measure.

Refinements of HDI

The UN now produces alternative indices and data to reflect some of the problems highlighted above. They include:

GDI (Gender-related Development Index)

The GDI reflects differences in male and female attainment and opportunities and deflates countries' rakings according to gender gaps.

GEM (Gender Empowerment Measure)

The GEM extends the GDI's data on opportunity to examine the use of equality: the extent to which women as well as men can engage in economic and political activity.

HPI (Human Poverty Index)

The HPI is a 'reverse' measure of development and examines lack of access to public and private services as well as low life expectancy and poor education as a measure of poverty.

Data on regions within countries

The UN provides and assesses data from different areas *within* an economy to advise on regional policy and target the most needy in the population.

What is a developing country?

The term developing country (or LEDC: less economically developed country) is a term used frequently to describe economies as diverse as Algeria, Barbados and Armenia.

A developing country is neither a developed economy (high HDI, high income per capita, usually highly industrialised or post-industrial in terms of employment and output) nor a failed state (very low HDI, stagnant economic and social well-being, weak or collapsed government). The term 'developing' therefore covers a wide range of countries on every continent, often with very different societies and industrial structures. The key characteristics of a developing country may be summarised as:

▶ Low and unequal income resulting in widespread poverty, poor health and possibly malnutrition

▶ High population growth with low life expectancy

▶ Low productivity levels (linked to low levels of educational attainment), with high unemployment or underemployment

▶ Lack of diversification in agricultural industrial output

Newly-industrialising countries (NICs) are often distinguished from other developing countries by their expanding levels of industrial output and, usually, growing importance in the pattern of global trade.

Why are some countries more developed than others?

This simple question lies at the heart of global poverty. We can identify some of the following as reasons why some countries are richer than others:

Resource endowment: the quantity and quality of factors of production

The link between inputs and output is central to economics. The quantity of factors available is important (100 million workers can produce more than 10 million workers, ceteris paribus), but richer countries tend to enjoy higher quality resources (more fertile land, more highly skilled workers, more efficient technology and more effective management) then poorer countries. The quality of resources is also crucial in determining productivity and thus GDP per capita.

Primary product dependency and worsening terms of trade

Developing countries (as do most countries before experiencing industrial revolution) tend to focus employment and output in the primary sector, i.e. extractive and agricultural industries. Mining, fishing and farming do not require huge levels of human capital and some developing countries enjoy factor endowments of a favourable climate or reserves of oil or gas. Comparative advantage theory proposes that gains from trade are derived from the exploitation of these endowments, but there may be dynamic costs

involved. The prices of agricultural commodities can be volatile in the short-run and, in the long-run, have not tended to rise in line with prices in the secondary and tertiary sectors. This represents a worsening of the **terms of trade** for developing countries. The terms of trade are the ratio of export prices to import prices. If an economy is exporting wheat and importing tractors, the terms of trade decline whenever the price of tractors rises faster than the price of wheat.

Poor infrastructure

Infrastructure describes the transport, communication and energy networks which are essential to get factors to their best use, and output to the geographical location where it can achieve its highest market value. Poor infrastructure therefore reduces potential output and leads to wasted time and, in the case of perishable goods, wasted output. Links to international infrastructure are also crucial for a country to fully gain from trading opportunities in world markets.

Human capital and population issues

The HDI focuses one third of its attention on educational attainment and the value it adds to peoples' lives. Education is crucial to growth and development both in a specific sense (gaining expertise for work: human capital) and a general sense (knowledge about health and hygiene, political, social and environmental implications of choice and opportunity, and personal cultural and intellectual enrichment). Rich countries tend to enjoy very high levels of adult literacy and compulsory education into the later teenage years, with possible exceptions where particular minority groups are excluded from such opportunities. Education regarding contraception is also crucial in avoiding rapid population growth which lowers the living standards of all. Such education may be particularly important where traditional cultural or religious beliefs contradict the economic good sense of small families.

Institutions, governments and corruption

Maintenance of law and order through good government is crucial if households and entrepreneurs are to see the value of long-run investment in education, personal healthcare, and human and physical capital. Economies where factors of production and the proceeds of economic activity may be appropriated by the government (or others) on an unpredictable basis do not provide an environment where there is sufficient trust and security to build strong economic growth over time. It is not surprising that regions where civil wars and terrorist activity persist over time tend to see the stagnation or even destruction of (usually already very scarce) factors of production.

Financial and currency constraints, the savings gap and debt

In developing countries there tends to be a lack of financial capital as a much higher proportion of household income is spent on basic necessities. This shortage of savings (sometimes called a **savings gap**), as well as limited formal and stable banking mechanisms, means there are limited funds available for investment, both private and public: entrepreneurs lack the funds to buy up to date technology, and governments find it difficult to make necessary improvements to infrastructure.

One option is for a government to fund investment themselves, but this can be simply the process of printing money and high levels of inflation may result (e.g. Zimbabwe). Alternatively, entrepreneurs and government may look overseas to developed economies to borrow money. The issue of Third World Debt has become a major issue in international finance and, despite a number of high profile pledges to write off such debt and free struggling economies from often punitive interest rates, many developed economies are still constrained by past borrowing and the conditions of such loans. This is particularly difficult when the terms of trade are declining for a country, and a higher and higher proportion of domestic output must be sold to gain sufficient revenue to meet interest payments.

Capital flight and labour flight

One serious problem for developing countries is the outflow of capital and labour. The '**brain drain**' effect – where workers with the best education and skills move to more developed countries where their human capital is rewarded by higher pay and living standards – can leave skills gaps and stagnant productivity levels in their 'home nation'.

Stages of economic development

The different sectors of an economy can be defined as *primary* (extractive and agricultural industries), *secondary* (manufacturing), *tertiary* (services) and *quaternary* (information and communication technologies) and many developed economies have followed a rough pattern where the dominant employer and producer has been each of these sectors in turn.

Similarly, the Rostow model of growth identified the move from a *traditional society* (high levels of subsistence farming) through *pre-conditions for take-off* (growth of mining and organised, mechanised farming), *take-off* (industrialisation), the *drive to maturity* (diversification of industry and increased distribution of wealth) to the *age of mass high consumption* (developed economy with strong tertiary and, increasingly, quaternary sectors).

In items of population the Demographic Transition Model provides another series of stages through which economies typically move over time.

Stage One: A high birth rate and high death rate, hence a broadly stable population with low life expectancy.

Stage Two: A high birth rate and a falling death rate, hence a growing population and a rising life expectancy.

Stage Three: A falling birth rate and death rate, resulting in a slowdown in population growth.

Stage Four: A low birth rate and death rate, hence a stable population with high life expectancy.

We can add a Stage Five in recent years where a falling birth rate, typically where average family size falls below two children, combines with a falling death rate (due to improvements in healthcare in key diseases such as cancer) to create **an ageing population**. Concerns over Stage Five of the model focus on the drain on tax revenues of old age pensions and the costs of nursing and healthcare in an increasingly elderly population. Unless the quantity of life is matched by higher quality of life (lower susceptibility of illness, and perhaps a longer average working life) the younger generations may well find themselves paying higher and higher levels of tax to fund this shortfall.

Other models of development focus on structural change (e.g. Lewis, who examined differences in productivity between rural and urban sectors of the economy) and the link between savings and investment (e.g. Harrod-Domar).

Policies to promote development

A key issue is the role of the private sector (firms providing goods and services motivated by profit) and the role of government supplying public goods. The provision or improvement of public goods such as law and order, or transport infrastructure, may best be achieved through government intervention. However, government failure can arise, particularly where there is the possibility of corruption (Public Choice Theory offers an insight into the problems arising when a government does not attempt to maximise social welfare, but rather pursues personal agendas or tries to buy votes with unfair policies). The private sector's contribution will be most effective where there is already a stable economic and political environment, reasonably high levels of human capital and openness to trade. This latter aspect is important as a country's broad strategy can be regarded as inward or outward looking. Examples of an **outward-looking strategy** is the greater openness to trade in China in recent years – with dramatic impacts on growth, employment structure and the environment.

The alternative strategy – inward-looking – is now discredited. But as we saw in Chapter 7 not every country is a winner in a globalised world.

Policies – and in some cases pre-conditions for development – include:

Macroeconomic stability (demand management)

High levels of inflation and unemployment reduce the long-run productive capacity of the economy through reducing investment, international competitiveness and the process of hysteresis (where human capital is lost through successive recessions in the economic cycle). This may be particularly true for a developing country where a lack of diversified output exposes the economy to the threat of exogenous shocks.

Public expenditure and supply-side growth

Government can promote long-run growth and development by spending tax revenues on factors which will promote human capital such as education and training. This is true for the most as well as the least developed economies. Higher productivity shifts the Long Run Aggregate Supply Curve and the Production Possibility Frontier outwards, and providing these gains are sustained and can build over successive time periods, development may arise.

Agriculture

Adding value to agricultural output is crucial unless the food produced is rare and therefore enjoys a premium price among richer consumers. One possibility for agriculture-based economies is to process, can or bottle their own produce and develop the marketing of their own brands.

Industrialisation and diversification

This has been the route chosen by NICs (Newly-Industrialising Countries) such as Singapore, Mexico and Malaysia, who have taken advantage of low labour costs and the availability of cheap land to compete directly with the developed countries in international markets for manufactured goods. Low costs have outweighed the transport costs resulting from geographical distance from high value markets to allow significant exploitation of comparative advantage.

Tourism

Some economies do not have suitable factor endowments to compete in the markets for manufactured goods. Countries and regions with pleasant climates and attractive scenery may choose instead to exploit their comparative advantage in tourism, particularly in attracting visitors from richer countries. High value can be added to, say, local beverages and handicrafts when sold to Western tourists, and economies such as Mauritius, Kenya and Thailand have thriving tourism industries.

Tourism requires a stable society with low levels of crime (at least in areas experienced by tourists) and good infrastructure. As with industrialisation, therefore, this is only a suitable route to development for a country already enjoying a reasonable standard of living.

Patterns of tourism can be volatile, however, and particularly vulnerable to problems such as social unrest or civil war. Sri Lanka illustrates this problem. Kenya seems certain to see fewer tourists after the violent protests at the beginning of 2008 following the disputed General Election result.

Aid and Debt

Aid is a controversial issue. It is important to distinguish between humanitarian aid, which is offered at the time of drastic human need (for example after a natural disaster) and development aid, which is linked more closely to the promotion and funding of economic development.

Of the two types of aid, development aid is more likely to carry direct or indirect economic or political burdens. In recent years there have been sustained efforts to write off debt owed by developing countries, but this has often been subject to certain conditions. Typical requirements for the receipt or the write-off of debt include:

(a) privatisation and market reforms

(b) macroeconomic stability, including fiscal discipline and tax reforms

(c) devaluation of the domestic currency

(d) policies to reduce poverty

(e) liberalisation on foreign direct investment inflows

Although each of the above may appear reasonable, critics have highlighted the benefits they bring to developed as well as developing countries. For example, weaker currencies allow cheaper imports of their commodities and goods into richer countries (which may be regarded as both an opportunity or a threat to the West) and liberalising investment flows allows multinational companies greater opportunities (and therefore greater opportunities to exploit workers and the environment?) in developing and newly industrialising countries.

In addition, the emphasis on free markets is seen by some as an insidious promotion of Western-style economics, which may not be relevant to all countries and regions.

The role of international institutions and fair trade

We noted in Chapter 7 of the roles of the IMF, World Bank and WTO. As with the point above on debt and aid, the power of these institutions causes concern to some who see the 'Washington consensus' on economic policy-making as biased and beneficial towards the hegemony of developed countries.

The so-called dependence theory argues that the concentration of wealth in developed countries requires – or *depends* on – exploitable opportunities and resources in the developing world. In this context dependence theorists argue that UN and US institutions are biased and actually propagate disadvantage in the developing world; they therefore support underdevelopment whilst pretending to reduce it.

Fair trade promotes the ethical treatment of workers in developing countries by paying a fair price (which, if not comparable to prices in developed countries, is at least higher than an 'exploitative' price which might be paid to a worker with few rights and no bargaining or market power) for output. There are also

It is important to distinguish between humanitarian aid offered in time of drastic human need and development aid.

initiatives to provide commercial and economic education to vulnerable workers. Critics of free trade target the subsidy effect of these higher prices (which may hold back, rather than promote development) and the failure of such a microeconomic process to tackle inequities in global markets.

Secure property rights

Property rights give holders a legal entitlement to exclusively exploit, for example, the land on which they live. In many developing economies property rights may be insecure, particularly where farming takes place on common land or there are arbitrary redistributions of ownership by the government or others. Economists such as Hernando de Soto have highlighted the importance of state protection of property rights to land and intellectual output, and suitable punishment for offenders. Clear ownership of land can also allow households to borrow money using their property as collateral (i.e. take out a mortgage) which can be used to invest. This may be linked to microfinance initiatives in developing countries where loans of small sums (typically less than US$100) are provided to entrepreneurs in developing countries. This latter approach was promoted by the Nobel prize-winner Muhammad Yunus through the Grameen Bank.

Sustainable economic development

Economic activity has an impact on the social and physical environment as well as on population structure and the distribution of income and wealth. The typical side-effects of growth are widening inequality and increased environmental depletion and degradation (see Chapter 3 on the Kuznets curves). Industrialisation and urbanisation have dramatic impacts on society, some of which may be regarded as undesirable. Sustainable economic growth and development takes place when standards of living rise without damaging the environment. It can be measured using the Index of Sustainable Economic Welfare (ISEW). ISEW can be calculated as the sum of consumption, investment, government spending, and unpaid domestic services (e.g. housework) minus private and public spending on defence and costs resulting from environmental damage.

Environmental economists use the term **natural capital** to describe the productive (in the widest sense, from timber and oil to beautiful scenery and wildlife) importance of natural resources. If externalities pertaining to environmental degradation and depletion are ignored, exporters in developing countries are effectively subsidising importers by undervaluing their own output. This has obvious implications for the terms of trade, but may also reduce productive capacity in the long-run. Persuading and allowing developing economies to make long-term rational decisions, when poverty and low life expectancy are of immediate concern, is a serious challenge for the world economy.

The ISEW therefore aims to offer a more accurate picture of social welfare than GDP per capita or the HDI. However, despite campaigns by (amongst others) Friends of the Earth, the main measures of economic well being used by governments and international policy-makers remain GDP (per capita) and the Human Development Index.

The costs of environmental impacts resulting from consumption and production are of increasing concern and interest to economists. They are explored further in our final Chapter in relation to the Stern Review on climate change.

Summary questions

1. What do we mean by development? How might we distinguish a developed country (or MEDC: More Economically Developed Country) from a developing country (or LEDC: Less Economically Developed Country)?

2. What are the strengths of the Human Development Index when compared to GDP data? Does it still suffer from some limitations?

3. Why are some economies more developed than others? Use examples to illustrate your answer.

4. What can be done to increase development? Will one set of policies be relevant to all cases of underdevelopment?

5. Why is sustainability of interest to economists? Does sustainable growth always mean lower growth?

Extension questions

A. Using HDI data available from the internet (e.g. www.hdr.undp.org) find anomalies in the rankings of 3 countries of your choice. What can explain these differences? What other information and data would help to 'adjust' these measures to reflect the experiences of everyday people in these countries?

B. Evaluate the importance of international institutions and developed countries in helping developing countries to develop.

C. Using your knowledge of GDP, HDI and ISEW, list other possible variables which could be used to assess the happiness or social welfare levels in an economy. What weighting would you give to each of the components you propose? Why may some people disagree with your choice?

Chapter 10

Challenges for the Global Economy

Global economy, global poverty?

At the heart of economics is the apparently simple problem of what to produce, how to produce it and who to produce it for. Adam Smith identified the importance of specialisation, or the division of labour, in *The Wealth of Nations* in 1776. The phenomenon of globalisation can be seen as an exercise in increasing specialisation on a global level as countries and regions attempt to maximise their gains from comparative advantage. Trade theory explains the mutual gains from specialisation and trade – the win-win outcome even where one country has absolute advantage in all industries.

Greater free trade thus offers the theoretical possibility of increasing living standards and reducing poverty levels across the world. Yet data suggests that inequality is actually increasing, not only between the richest and poorest nations, but also within most nations. A UN report in 2005 stressed the importance of economic development rather than economic growth in reducing poverty. Better healthcare, wider access to education, and serious attempts to prevent the marginalisation of specific groups are needed if the citizens of developing countries are to avoid seeing their living standards fall further behind richer households in both their own countries and in the developed world.

The 1990 Human Development Report began with the statement, "People are the real wealth of a nation." Economics in the real world is fascinating not because it examines behaviour on both a micro and macro level, but because the small scale and the aggregate are so clearly interconnected.

Good (and bad) news travels fast...

Globalisation is characterised by faster communication, travel and transport. The speed with which business orders, innovations and good management practice can move is increasing, but so too is the spread of less positive events such as financial crises, falling confidence and economic downturn. Recent years have been a challenging time for the world economy, and this chapter will explore some of the main trends and issues emerging – and relate them to economic theories from previous chapters.

The Credit Crunch: markets for borrowing and lending

Extensive lending in the US housing market – and in particular the so-called subprime lending (loans made to higher risk borrowers) – caused alarm in financial markets across the world as the risks involved were bundled into complex financial instruments. This raised risk premiums for lending and the resulting shortage of funds (or lack of liquidity) caused a shortage of credit for households and firms alike, pushing up interest rates even when base rates had been cut.

The 'Credit Crunch' and resulting recession highlighted the growing interdependence between national financial markets. In theory, the ability of investors and lenders to diversify risks across a wider geographical area should help to stabilise the world financial sector. Thus even if returns are declining in, say, Europe, funds can be transferred to assets in areas where growth and potential profits are higher. However, this analysis makes the assumption that different sectors and areas of the world economy grow at different rates, and that downturn in one region may be outweighed by upturn somewhere else. If this is not true, and financial cycles are converging and losing independence, it may have serious consequences for anyone trying to find opportunities for diversification.

Global economic slowdown

We have already discussed the problems facing some of the more highly-indebted European nations in Chapter 8, but the global slowdown and recession at the end of the 2000s pushed even large economies such as the USA and UK into negative growth and fiscal crisis. Large bailouts and even nationalisation of some of the financial sector placed additional pressure on government finances at a time when the automatic stabilisers of falling tax revenues and rising welfare payments were increasing budget deficits. The multiplier-accelerator theory explained in Chapter 1 shows how an initial slowdown resulting from an exogenous shock can feed through to create a deep recession.

BRIC and world growth

With the threat of slower growth in traditionally dominant economies such as USA and those in Western Europe, the importance of four countries which we can identify with the acronym BRIC – Brazil, Russia, India and China (especially important) as sources of global economic growth will increase.

Some macroeconomic data on those economies is shown in Table 10.1.

Table 10.1: Macroeconomic data for BRIC countries, July 2011

	GDP Growth (%)	Inflation (%)	Unemploy-ment (%)	Current Account (% GDP)	Budget Balance (% GDP)
Brazil	4.2	6.6	6.4	- 2.7	-2.1
Russia	4.1	9.6	6.4	+ 4.8	-1.5
India	7.8	9.1	10.8	-3.4	-4.8
China	9.7	5.5	6.1	+ 3.6	-2.1

Source: *The Economist*

If economic growth in the BRIC nations is high by Western standards, so perhaps are the inflation rates. The extent to which this is demand-pull (reflecting higher incomes and wealth) or cost-push (implying bottlenecks in the supply process) may determine how well these economies can continue to provide cheap factors of production and goods and services to the world economy. China, in particular, and Brazil appear to have available workers but their productivity could be limited by structural factors.

It is also worth noting that all four of the BRIC economies are currently running a budget deficit (although all at levels enviable from a UK perspective) and, perhaps surprisingly, both Brazil and India are experiencing a current account deficit.

A simplistic view of world trade is that the East produces and exports and the West imports and consumes. However, the latest data shows that Western demand is no longer the driver for export sales. For Singapore, the rest of Asia is a much bigger export market than the EU or the USA. Even for the USA, developing Asia is now a larger export market than Germany. The UK, however, depends far more on sales in the USA and the rest of the EU than other EU countries. Developing wider and deeper trading links with faster growing economies has to be a key challenge for the UK economy if it is to drive export growth and consequently aggregate demand in the years ahead.

Whether emerging economies such as BRIC are sufficiently 'decoupled' from weak growth and financial problems in the USA will be an important factor in determining the progress of the world economy in the years ahead.

The UK economy: the party is over

The UK was hit hard by the recession of 2008-2009 and the key issues now facing the UK economy are high and growing government debt and an apparently fragile recovery. The government and Bank of

Figure 10.1: GDP growth (quarterly, % year-on-year)

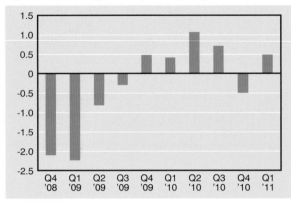

Source: HM Treasury

Figure 10.2: UK net debt (% GDP)

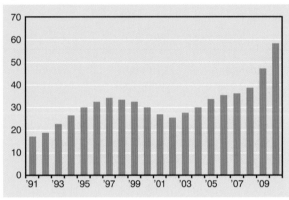

Source: HM Treasury

England face a dilemma: closing the budget deficit too slowly will increase interest payments on national debt, further cutting into tax revenue and forcing spending even lower and debt even higher; but on the other hand more drastic corrections to the fiscal stance may have a downward multiplier effect strong enough to push the economy back into recession. Figure 10.1 shows just how fragile the recovery has been. Quarterly data shows how Q4 of 2010 saw GDP contract by 0.5%. The economy grew again in Q1 of 2011, and so technically a recession did not recur (this would have required two consecutive periods of negative economic growth).

It is significant to note that the UK government abandoned its own fiscal rules (which allowed only an excess of capital, not current spending against tax revenues over the economic cycle, and a constraint on national debt to a maximum of 40% of GDP in any given year) when it became apparent they would be impossible to stick to in the face of global economic crisis.

Sustainable economic growth and development

A different form of sustainability was highlighted in the Stern Review on the *Economics of Climate Change* in October 2006. This was the first major study of the economic impact of global warming, and the conclusions offered made bleak reading. Stern offered a simple choice: sacrifice 1% of global GDP in the immediate term, or face a long-term drop of 20% in global GDP. The 1% must be invested, he argued, to invest in cleaner technologies and more environmentally sustainable lifestyles and infrastructure.

The Stern Review prompted considerable controversy not least because of its implications for those economies which enjoy high levels of consumer spending, air travel and private car use. There has been considerable criticism regarding the statistical assumptions and analysis used. Nonetheless, the Stern Review may prove most beneficial not for its predictive accuracy, but for opening the debate and quantifying the benefits and costs of dealing with the environmental changes which have been magnified by increased industrialisation, urbanisation and rising standards of living across the globe.

The key problem to tackling climate change is the need for international consensus. As of July 2011, 192 states had ratified the Kyoto protocol, an agreement to reduce greenhouse gas emissions. However, the USA does not feature amongst this large number of countries and so has not ratified the treaty. Without full agreement from major world powers, prospects for averting further damage to the environment seem bleak.

Protectionism?

There are two main criticisms of globalisation:

(a) Globalisation reduces living standards in developed countries

(b) Globalisation reduces living standards in developing countries

These arguments both contradict the theoretical gains proposed by free trade theory. Argument (a) is often used to justify protectionism in developed countries, where it may be felt that domestic jobs and output are being undermined by cheap imports from abroad. This factor may slow down the globalisation process in the future. The expansion and strengthening of customs unions such as the European Union may be seen as a 'second best' response to the high levels of competition emerging from NICs; members enjoy the benefits of free trade with similar economies which are unlikely to outcompete each other in all markets, whilst enjoying unilateral protection against lower cost producers outside the union.

Argument (b) often arises from such protectionism. The Doha Development Round, which began in 2001 and is still underway, aims to lower barriers to trade, particularly those which are seen as biased against developing countries. The Common Agricultural Policy of the EU protects the jobs and incomes of European farmers and keeps food prices high within the EU (which also harms consumers) and excludes cheaper imports from the developing world. The power of developed countries to influence international institutions and negotiations is seen as a major problem in providing an export-led escape from poverty and underdevelopment in many countries in the world.

Monetary policy, too, has been under strain with the UK base rate retained at 0.5% despite the official CPI measure of inflation rising as high as 4.4% in February 2011. The Bank of England is also trying to balance control of a key measure of economic performance against the uncertainty of future growth.

It is inevitable and obvious that the UK faces years of much slower growth than that experienced during the NICE decade. Some economists have dubbed this period the hangover after the party, as the UK economy works through problems stored up by excessive speculation and unsustainable growth during the 'good times.' The UK economy is not alone – many economies face similar problems, if not worse. What is extremely likely is that the next decade will see the pattern of global economic power shift considerably, and in ways impossible to predict.

Table 10.1: The World Economy in 2010 – latest data

Population	7 billion people
GDP	$60 trillion (2010 estimate)
GDP per capita	$7 000
Annual GDP per capita growth	-0.8% (2009 estimate)
People earning less than $2 per day	3.25 billion
Number of millionaires	10 million
Number of billionaires	1,000
Number of mobile phones (2007 data)	3.3 billion
Number of airports (2004 data)	50,000
Roads (2004 data)	Over 30 million km
Railways (2004 data)	Over 1 million km
Military Expenditure (1998 data)	$750 billion (2% of global GDP)

Summary questions

1. What are the most pressing issues facing the UK economy at present?
2. What are the most pressing issues facing the world economy at present?
3. "Significantly closing the gap between developed and developing economies will reduce comparative advantages, and thus reduce potential gains from trade." Carefully explain this reasoning.
4. Explain why the UK authorities face problems in setting both fiscal and monetary policy given the prevailing economic conditions.
5. To what extent is full international co-operation necessary to tackle climate change?

Extension questions

A. Is a lack of development in an economy a result of market failure or government failure?
B. What issues merit the most attention from economists in the 21st century?
C. Evaluate the effectiveness of economics, alone, in tackling the issues you have mentioned in B.

Index